A MEMORY OF FIRELIGHT

A Memory of Firelight

Selected Columns
From The Lexington Herald-Leader

Paul Prather

WIND PUBLICATIONS

International Standard Book Number 978-1-936138-01-2
Library of Congress Control Number 2009932611

First edition

The author acknowledges with grateful appreciation the cooperation of the *Lexington Herald-Leader* in the production of this book.

This book is for Harper.
I hope that through it she'll eventually understand
where she came from, and realize how many people
have loved her appearing.

CONTENTS

INTRODUCTION

I began writing newspaper columns twenty years ago, shortly after joining the *Lexington Herald-Leader* as a cub reporter. On the rare occasions there wasn't much happening on my real beat covering various Kentucky businesses, I'd knock out those early personal essays in my spare time, every few months. Mainly, my early columns were humorous pieces about my childhood or my experiences as a father.

After two years as a business reporter, I became the *Herald-Leader*'s religion writer. That entailed a move to the features department. (Newsroom wags pointed out that my transfer from the business desk to the religion beat wasn't much of a leap.)

The features editor, Paula Anderson, had enjoyed my earlier, sporadic columns and asked me to produce an opinion piece each week about issues facing Kentucky's faith communities, such as the conservative takeover of the Southern Baptist Convention or the debate over whether Catholic priests ought to marry. She said I could write these in addition to my duties as a reporter of straightforward religion-news stories.

Demagogue that I aspire to be, I instantly embraced the idea of having a weekly dais from which to browbeat the masses. Still, I figured there was no opinion I could express on religion without causing a large portion of my audience to go stark raving berserk. People feel strongly about their churches or even about their lack thereof. If I were to praise, say, Methodists, I might cause them momentarily to love me—but would incur the wrath of Episcopalians, Jews, Baptists or agnostics.

I was surprised when these opinion pieces turned out to be popular. Certainly I got my share of criticism, but the positive responses outnumbered the negative.

So I continued to wax mediocre on any number of spiritual topics until I left the newspaper in 1997 to become a full-time minister. I'd already been a bi-vocational pastor for years, tapping a newsroom keyboard on weekdays and preaching on Sundays. My church in Montgomery County had developed into a full-time job of its own.

Then, in 2000, three years into my journalistic "retirement," my wife, Renee, fell ill. By the time it was diagnosed, her cancer had spread through both her breasts and into her bones, lungs and, doctors suspected, liver. After grim talks with a surgeon and an oncologist, Renee and I discussed our options. The surgeon had said the cancer was inoperable. The oncologist had said we could try chemotherapy, but that there was, in his words, "zero chance" chemo would cure her, and not much chance it would even temporarily slow the disease's progress. Without chemo, he said, she couldn't live more than two months.

Renee and I agonized for days before deciding that if treatment couldn't heal her, and if it probably wouldn't even help—and if in the meantime it would cause her to feel sicker and lose her hair—she should forgo chemo and trust God.

She lived five years.

At first she was thin but looked otherwise healthy, and she briefly continued working at the branch bank where she was manager. Soon, though, she had to go on disability. I became her primary caregiver.

As time went on, Renee could hardly leave the house except for brief outings to church or to have her hair done. Later yet, she couldn't move around much even inside our home, barely hobbling from room to room. Nearer the end, she became bedfast.

In the midst of Renee's illness, in 2002, Todd Wethall, the editor of the *Lexington Herald-Leader*'s new Faith and Values section, approached me about writing a freelance column on spirituality, along the lines of what I'd done when I was a staff writer.

I didn't believe I could focus my mind enough to say anything coherent. But Todd only wanted one column a month. I decided it might be a good distraction, a form of therapy for which I'd get paid instead of having to pay someone else.

When I'd been a columnist before, readers had gotten to know me and my family. They knew that Renee and I had one of the happier marriages around, that she was the one who kept my feet planted on solid earth, since I was tempted to take fanciful flights. So in my first new piece, I explained Renee's condition, told what our lives were like now. At the bottom of the column, the *Herald-Leader* published my e-mail address.

The responses rolled in. I quit counting the e-mails when they topped 100. I also received many letters and cards. Readers stopped me at Wal-Mart or phoned my house.

Something about our family's struggles had hit a chord. After writing several columns about other subjects, I wrote a second piece about Renee's illness. Again, I was overwhelmed with responses.

It wasn't just that the volume of feedback increased when I wrote about Renee. I noticed a difference in the length and tone of the communications. People wrote me page after page, pouring out their hearts. Probably ninety percent of my correspondents were other caregivers. They told me about their sick loved ones, about their own fatigue, about how they'd begun to doubt God. It was as if they needed a safe place to vent.

And thus I wrote even more about our family's ordeals.

Those ordeals only seemed to worsen. In 2003, my mother was diagnosed with breast cancer. Doctors thought they'd caught her cancer early, that all Mom needed was a lumpectomy. Within two months— the amount of time our oncologist originally had given Renee—Mom was dead.

Two years later, Renee died.

After both Renee and my mother were gone, I told readers about my loneliness and regrets. By then, I was producing two columns a month. For a while, half my columns were on caregiving or grief. I hadn't set out to become a self-appointed expert on those subjects. But our family's losses were on my mind. And from the mail I was getting, I knew I'd stumbled upon an area of great need. I came to view those columns as a door of ministry God had opened, albeit a door I'd never wanted to walk through.

Writing each of those pieces was agonizing. Afterward, I'd fall into a funk for days. But I tried to I accept that Renee's sickness and death, and my mom's, might be, paradoxically, instruments of healing—healing of a kind we wouldn't have chosen, emotional healing for strangers we'd never meet.

Renee, I think, had foreseen that, or something near it. When she was sick, she used to tell me, "What we're going through isn't for us. What we're suffering, God is allowing so that it can help other people."

In any case, months went by, and then years. I made new discoveries. I began to date, spasmodically, tentatively. I found a steady girlfriend, Liz, and discovered again, in middle age, the myriad lessons of navigating a budding, serious relationship.

My son, John, finished college. He married. Right off the bat John's bride, Cassie, became pregnant. Learning I was going to become a grandpa—I received the news at my fifty-second birthday party—ranks among my life's happiest moments.

The *Herald-Leader*'s readers followed me, and like good friends cheered me on, through all these developments.

Today, I'm often invited to speak to civic groups, medical groups, colleges and churches. Invariably, people ask where they can get a collection of my columns.

I finally decided to suck it up, practice some self-discipline (which isn't among my inborn virtues) and put this book together. I'd planned to include a sampling from my whole twenty years as an on-again, off-again columnist. But when I tried to sort through the immense stack of gasbaggery I've written over that span, I found that paring it down required more diligence than I could muster, not to mention a stronger gag reflex.

I chose instead only from the columns I've produced during the past half-dozen years, since I started writing again for the *Herald-Leader*. That seemed manageable. And those years have constituted an interesting segment of my life: through Renee's illness and death, through my mother's sickness and passing, and on toward my own emotional and spiritual recovery.

I considered arranging these essays by topic—humor, politics, caregiving. But it seemed better to let them fall chronologically, which provides a clearer sense of my journey. I've tried to select the pieces that resonated most with readers or, barring that, the ones that still resonate with me.

I thank the various editors at the *Herald-Leader* who've been patient enough to read these columns and frequently improve them: Todd, Lu-Ann, Risa. I thank Charlie Hughes at Wind Publications for taking on this book project, and Linda Austin at the *Herald-Leader* for approving it.

I thank Liz Mandrell, my girlfriend, for her encouragement and proofreading skills. I thank John and Cassie for making me a grandpa to Harper.

I'm just grateful to be here, still standing, still writing. I'm not as energetic or optimistic as that young reporter who initially cranked out funny little essays in his spare time, but at least I'm consistent—two columns a month, come hell or high water. I've learned that if I can't do anything else, I can be faithful.

LONG ORDEAL SHOWS WHO
IS TRULY FAITHFUL

April 20, 2002

Two years ago, my wife, Renee, was diagnosed with advanced cancer. Her prognosis couldn't have been worse; her life expectancy was measured in weeks. She's still here, still more lucid than I am, still more full of hope.

Renee used to weigh 140 pounds. The last time she got on the scale, a year ago, she weighed eighty. She might have lost more since then, but she's not eager to find out.

Her world consists mainly of our den, where she passes her time lying in a hospital bed reading, cross-stitching or staring at Oprah on the TV.

I'm her full-time caretaker.

We have good days, but for the most part, her illness has been excruciating for both of us. Our previous, blissful life together has been laid waste.

I've learned a lot of valuable lessons, none of which I ever wanted to know.

For instance, right after Renee got sick, we were blessed with an enormous outpouring of concern from Christians in our community.

Fellow ministers came to our house and prophesied that Renee would be healed. Other people formed prayer chains. A few told Renee to repent of her supposed sins. Some recommended fruit and vegetable diets. They all had answers.

Heck, we tried a lot of their suggestions.

And Renee might recover yet. She believes she will. If cancer has sense enough to recognize my wife's stubbornness, it had better listen to her and run.

But in the meantime she's still sick—and we're still stuck. The television drones. Birthdays and holidays pass. Newspapers yellow with age.

Most of our well-meaning preachers and prophets don't come around anymore. They might have gotten distracted, or discouraged, or simply had to get on with business. All of which I've done to others.

As it turns out, the folks who have been the most comfort, who have saved our sanity, have not been the types of people who'd see themselves as spiritual powerhouses.

Every Tuesday, Renee's sister travels from Nicholasville to Mount Sterling to help with our housework and stay with Renee while I go to a movie or take a long drive in the country. I exist from one Tuesday to the next.

Sometimes, friends bring us home-cooked meals or restaurant carryout. We sit in the den and eat Thai food and talk. It's like living again.

My buddy Jim Jordan, a Herald-Leader business writer, e-mails me regularly with what he calls "Friday Funnies"—jokes to lift my spirits.

A handful of others perform similar good deeds.

So here's a lesson that, being a big-mouthed preacher myself, I wish I'd understood long before Renee got sick, and hope now to never, ever forget:

When you're suffering, you often feel forgotten, bewildered and faithless.

You discover that the person who shows up once to deliver a prophecy isn't necessarily the mightiest messenger of God, and sure isn't the one who eases your pain.

No, the truly anointed messenger is the one who arrives every week, for years, to scrub your toilet.

MEANING CAN BE FOUND
IN TRANSLATION

May 18, 2002

Sometimes people ask me whether I speak in tongues.

Yes, I do. Mainly my unknown tongue is preacher-talk, the impenetrable jargon we ministers employ to help us sound holy—and to mask our true thoughts.

But the Bible warns that it's worthless to speak in an obscure dialect unless you also can interpret the messages into a language others understand.

So let me offer some translations here.

It's the final night of my church's spring bowling league. The team I'm on, The Four Guys, is about to battle for the league championship against The Heavenly Bodies.

I wear my game face, not to mention my John Prine T-shirt, which always brings me good luck.

As I rub rosin on my bowling hand, I'm approached by a member of my congregation who's not involved in the title match. She has other, less important matters on her mind: She's been reading a book that says God sometimes forces Christians to suffer as a way of purifying us. She finds this idea disturbing.

"How can a loving God make us suffer?" she asks morosely.

WHAT I SAY: "God's grace is many-layered. We simply must trust his wisdom."

INTERPRETATION: "In about five minutes, you can watch The Heavenly Bodies suffer. We Four Guys are fixing to stomp their Heavenly heinies—in love, of course."

8

In the first game of our three-game series, the Four Guys—all of us middle-age ex-jocks who live to prove that, while there may be snow on our roofs (and guts over our belts), there's plenty of testosterone still percolating in our naughty regions—knock down every pin in sight: Strike, strike, spare, strike.

The Heavenly Bodies, usually a fine team, tonight couldn't hit the pocket with a bazooka. They couldn't knock down the head pin if they drove a logging truck down lane twelve. Karen, my sister-in-law, walks to the line to bowl for the Heavenlies, looking dejected.

WHAT I SAY: "I'm praying for you!"

INTERPRETATION: "Smite that infidel, O God, with the seven-ten split of thy wrath!"

The Four Guys win the first game by nearly sixty pins. In the next game we're even better. A manly whiff of testosterone floats on the air. Or maybe that's our BenGay.

I'm bowling a clean game—no open frames at all—on my way to a 200-plus score. One dude from the Heavenly Bodies calls out: "Pastor, are you taking steroids?"

WHAT I SAY: "No, my son, the Lord is blessing me."

INTERPRETATION: "I got my John-Prine-T-shirt mojo working."

We Four Guys win the first two games, throw away the third, but take total pinfall for the evening's series. We're the undisputed champs. Easily.

I shake hands with each of the Heavenly Bodies. I pat their shoulders.

WHAT I SAY: "It's only a game. What does it matter in the scope of eternity?"

INTERPRETATION: "Eat mud and die, losers."

Demonstrating the fruit of the Spirit, I restrain my sudden impulse to dance the macarena on the Heavenly Bodies' table. Instead I turn to my teammates.

WHAT I SAY: "God is good, my brothers, all the time."

INTERPRETATION: "Middle age can kiss our bowling shoes! We're still four baaaaad men!"

FLAWED DELIVERERS
BRING GOD'S MESSAGE

June 29, 2002

When I was a boy, my father gave altar calls at the close of almost every sermon he preached.

I stood countless times as congregations warbled "Just As I Am," the invitational hymn. My dad would plead with sinners to surrender their hearts to Jesus and for lukewarm Christians to rededicate their lives.

Often as I stared down the aisle at my father wearing his Sears suit, issuing his appeal—"If you come, we'll sing one more verse; if no one comes, this verse will close the invitation"—I found myself nearly overwhelmed with melancholy.

Dad looked so small and vulnerable. I'd grip the back of a pew to keep from running to him. I didn't want to repent; I just wanted to hug him. I didn't understand why.

Ironically, today I'm a pastor. Dad and I minister in the same church.

I don't give many altar calls, but I do preach, offering up my thoughts about redemption and error. My father and my son watch me.

And as I speak, I feel paltry.

I suspect that nearly every man or woman who has stood before any congregation of any religion in any age would recognize that sensation. But it might be something you folks who sit in the pews—or stay home in bed—don't know about us.

We ministers have spent much of our lives doing and thinking all the things everyone else does. We've rooted for the Cats, lusted for sex, boogied to Bob Seger and endured the flu. We're as human as they come, every bit as silly and vain.

Then, through a confluence of circumstances—the calling of God, peer pressure, hubris, whatever—we discover ourselves dressed in Sunday clothes, facing 100 sets of eyes, presuming to tell others the unknowable.

There exists a God, his followers say, who is so immense the universe can't hold him, so wise the philosophers can't comprehend him, so powerful the demons of hell can't defeat him. He remains invisible and stone silent.

And there we stand, trying to speak on his behalf.

We look at all those eyes looking back at us and realize we're rattling on about the fates of our listeners' immortal souls. The message is cosmically huge, the stakes are incredibly high—and we, the messengers, are so woefully frail.

We ought to shut up, but we can't, because the words spill out despite us. God is performing the magic trick he works a million times a week, in every nation: He's talking through clay.

We hope. Or perhaps we're just gasbags.

Even as a boy, I sensed that my father was inadequate for such a job.

So am I. So are you.

That's what it means to be a preacher. At least that's my experience of it. I wouldn't give you a dime for any minister who thinks he's up to the task.

One day, I have an ugly wart cut off my scalp; the next day I proclaim the Incarnation. I dash to the church restroom to comb my hair or urinate or check for food in my crooked teeth, then hurry out to explain the resurrection of a guy who'd been dead three days and who, oh yeah, happened to be the savior of humanity.

I've chosen, or been chosen (as the case may be), to serve as a mouthpiece for the Almighty. It leaves me feeling like a saint occasionally, and like an imbecile mostly.

AMID PAIN OF CANCER,
IT HELPS TO LAUGH

July 20, 2002

A few months ago, I wrote about my family's ongoing struggle with my wife's advanced cancer.

I received many sympathetic e-mails and letters, for which I thank you all. But believe it or not, there is a lighter side to sickness. Renee, our son and I always have shared a twisted sense of humor:

For instance, Renee used to have a voluptuous figure. Now her chest is flat as a clipboard. (My wife let me write that.)

She and I are in the den watching the reality TV series "The Bachelor," in which several women compete for the affections of an eligible young man. I'm sitting on the sofa. Renee is lying in her leased hospital bed.

The bachelor interviews one woman who tells him she likes to dress up for "romance" in a Wonder Woman costume.

"Hey, honey," I say, "that's something you've never done. Let's buy you a Wonder Woman outfit."

She glances down at her body.

"If I wore it now," she says, "it would be a Wonder-Where-She-Went outfit."

It's a pleasant evening, and Renee is feeling comparatively strong. I load her in the car. We go for ice cream, then take a leisurely drive in the country with the windows down, enjoying the breeze and the chirps of crickets. This is a big night out for us.

Near midnight, I finally turn our car into the cul-de-sac where we live—and see something in the shadows, darting off the street into our driveway.

I pull alongside this unidentified moving object. It's our son, nineteen, burning rubber in his mother's wheelchair.

"John, what are you doing?" I say.

"Popping wheelies," he says. "This chair is bad."

A few days later, I'm preparing to leave for a writers' conference in Maryland. I help Renee pack so she can stay with one of her sisters while I'm gone.

John will have the house to himself for several days.

He enters the room, looks around at the gear I've collected for Renee, purses his lips as if trying to choose his words carefully.

"Uh, Mom," he says finally. "You're not, uh, taking the wheelchair, are you?"

Disease has affected Renee's vocal chords. At forty-one, she sounds like a seven-year-old child, which irritates her to no end.

Yet she keeps our cordless phone on the bed beside her. It's one of her few links to the outside world; she's always the first to answer calls.

Unfortunately we still attract telemarketers, the new antisolicitation law notwithstanding.

The phone rings.

Renee: "Hello?"

She pauses, frowns.

"No, you can't," she squeaks.

Pause.

"Because my daddy doesn't live here."

Pause.

"My mommy doesn't live here, either."

Pause.

"Would you like to speak to my man?"

Long pause.

Renee holds the phone in the air, arches an eyebrow toward me.

"I guess he didn't want to talk to you."

Hey, you might as well laugh. It definitely beats crying. We know that for a fact.

AFTER TWENTY YEARS, THIS MINISTER
KNOWS A LITTLE SOMETHING

August 17, 2002

I first became a pastor in 1982, at a thirty-member church in Montgomery County, Kentucky.

I'm grayer now, and crankier, and have more people to look after, but I'm still pastoring, in fact just a couple of miles down the highway from where I started. Several of those original thirty are still with me.

I'm no superstar. I'm a journeyman. But if you do anything for twenty years, you learn lessons about it, whether it's laying bricks or leading a congregation. Here are a few insights about the ministry that I've gleaned from experience:

• I don't know much. When I started, I saw every issue in stark blacks and whites: baptism, divorce, administration, Scripture, Communion, sin, heaven, hell. You name it, I had the answer. Today, my opinions are about as gray as my hair. Life and religion have turned out to be not nearly as clear-cut as I would have preferred.

• You can fall out of a canoe on either side. People who are extremists on one side of an issue are about as prone to disaster as those who are extremists on the other side. For instance, if you believe God never performs miracles today, you're going to cheat yourself out of many blessings. But if you believe he's duty-bound to dole out a miracle every time you're in a mess, you're going to lose your faith completely.

• When you're dealing with people, what you see is what you get. People can seem heaven-sent one week—they're volunteering in Sunday school or mending the sanctuary roof—and be long gone by the

14

next week. Enjoy them today, while you've got them, then turn them loose. In the Lord's work, no one is irreplaceable. Including you.

• We ministers get to deal with the cream of the crop. The last point notwithstanding, many of the people we encounter in churches are a truly cut above the society as a whole. They're more polite, more loyal, more honest, more charitable.

• Generally, no single day makes or breaks you (unless it's the day you sucker-punch the chairman of the deacons). I've preached a few great sermons—and a hundred gosh-awful ones. Here's what they have in common: None of them individually made much difference. People mainly are affected by the cumulative tone of your ministry during the long haul, not by any particular episode.

• Similarly, the details rarely matter. In the scope of eternity, it's inconsequential whether the basement renovation gets finished on time or a month late. It doesn't matter whether the choir robes are trimmed in green or blue—or whether you have choir robes. You don't even have to have a choir.

• Most people who claim to have heard directly from God haven't. Don't allow folks to intimidate you as a leader because they've got some hot new revelation. They probably don't. On the other hand, do listen. Because once in a while, someone really does receive a word from the Lord. Your job is to discern the difference.

• Even for ministers, the gospel is the simplest message on Earth. It boils down to principles a kindergartener could understand: love them all, and forgive them all; if you do that, God will love and forgive you. It's simple, but it's not easy.

People will overlook almost any fault a pastor has if they know he or she genuinely loves them. Call people when they're sick, rejoice when they get a promotion, commiserate with their frustrations about their kids—and many of them will become your brothers and sisters for life.

TIME CATCHES UP, THEN PASSES US BY

August 31, 2002

Religion is filled with incalculable mysteries. But there is no mystery more baffling to me than that of time.

We humans love to believe we are eternal beings created by an eternal God. And yet all our feeble lives, we are victims of a ticking clock.

When I was a teenager, my elderly grandfather suffered a bout with what in those days was diagnosed as "hardening of the arteries." For a short period, he was disoriented and hallucinating.

My father, then middle-age, sat up with him in the hospital.

Papa, who'd always been an outdoorsman, thought he was hunting. He berated Dad for making too much noise, then felt sorry and apologized: "I didn't aim to be hateful with you, son, but you were scaring off the squirrels."

Papa's mind returned, and he lived several more years in decent health.

Recently my dad, now in his seventies, was hospitalized with symptoms similar to his dad's. He didn't see squirrels that weren't there, but he saw several people the rest of us couldn't see. Plus he'd go to the bathroom and couldn't find his way out.

At first the doctors thought he'd had a stroke. Ultimately, after conducting every test known to medical science, they decided they had no idea what had happened to him.

Fortunately he's back home and, as we used to say, "back at himself" mentally.

But for several days, my mother, sister and I sat with him in a hospital and listened as he talked nonsense. I tried to feed my father his supper.

It hit me how our roles had shifted. He'd nursed his father. Now I was nursing him. I have a boy roughly the same age as I was when my grandfather suffered his spell.

Later I tried to explain this to my son.

"See what you've got to look forward to?" I said. "Before you know it, you'll be watching me squirrel-hunt in my hospital room."

He laughed. I laughed. But it wasn't particularly funny.

I have a niece I used to hold in one hand by her ankles. I could let my arm dangle full-length and swing her, without her head bumping the floor. Now she's a married woman, a mother to three children.

I used to ride my son and nephew on my feet, both boys at the same time. Today each guy stands six-foot-three. Some days I do well to carry myself around on my feet.

It's been this way since Adam and Eve. We've got microwaves now and cell phones and satellite TVs and the Internet.

But the cycle never changes. People are conceived as seeds. They're born helpless. They grow tall and strong. They marry, create children of their own. They stoop. They fade. They slip into the ground. They are forgotten.

Time flows on. Another generation follows. And then another.

The late James Still explored this mystery in his classic novel *River of Earth*. In it a mountain minister, Brother Mobberly, says to his congregation:

"These hills are jist dirt waves, washing through eternity. My brethren, they hain't a hill standing so proud but hit'll sink to the low ground o' sorrow. Oh, my children, where air we going on this mighty river of earth, a-borning, begetting, and a-dying—the living and the dead riding the waters? Where air it sweeping us?"

The answer, of course, is that none of us knows. Only God can say.

ORIGINAL SIN IS INHERENT TO PARADISE

October 19, 2002

I recently spent a week in Bar Harbor, Maine, my favorite vacation spot. If there's a more beautiful or restful place on Earth, I've yet to find it. The weather was perfect: sunny, temperatures in the seventies, a gentle ocean breeze.

Deer wandered alongside the country roads of Acadia National Park as my brother-in-law, who accompanied me, and I took leisurely afternoon drives. The New England leaves were beginning to change to orange and regal shades of purple.

In the harbor itself, seals frolicked on crags. Lighthouses and lobster boats glowed golden in the sunsets. The sea was glass. The whole area looked like a postcard.

One day we took a ride on a lobster boat. What the captain told us about this paradise brought me back to reality—and to a spiritual paradox of our world.

Beneath the shimmering waters of Bar Harbor, an ongoing warfare is raging daily, a murderous struggle to survive by destroying all competitors.

As he hoisted a trap and took out a wriggling lobster, Captain John asked if we knew why in restaurants live lobsters have rubber bands fastened around their claws. We guessed that it was to keep the creatures from crushing the fingers of restaurant workers. Not really, the captain said. It's because lobsters are ruthless cannibals.

Lobstermen check each of their traps every day or two, he said, because if several lobsters end up in the same trap, the most powerful one will kill and eat the others. You'll pull up your cage and find a fat lobster surrounded by fragments of shell and scattered bits of antennae.

Same thing happens in a lobster tank in a restaurant, he said. Let one lobster break a rubber band and get a pincer free, and he'll make quick work of the others nearby.

My brother-in-law and I also toured a lobster hatchery. We saw female lobsters ripe with eggs bunched like caviar along the undersides of their tails.

A hatchery worker said that in the wild, of the 20,000 fertilized eggs a female carries, one in every 1,000 offspring actually makes it to adulthood. Most of the remaining 999 are eaten in infancy by other sea creatures.

That same week in Maine I picked up a copy of *The New York Times* that carried a science article about the lives of insects in a meadow near Henry David Thoreau's Walden Pond, and one on recent discoveries about pygmy octopuses, some of which are no bigger than a human thumbnail.

Under each fallen leaf near Walden, the *Times* reporter observed, exists a chaotic, lethal world. For example, the article said, "centipedes are predators as fearsome as saber-toothed tigers." Tiny rove beetles are similarly dangerous in their neighborhoods.

Back in the ocean, octopuses the size of jellybeans stalk coral crevices and, like "lions of miniature rain forests," prey constantly on "tiny shrimps, crabs or snails."

I listened to the lobster experts, read the *Times* and soon afterward watched on TV stories of a woman pummeling her child in a parking lot, of a mob of schoolchildren beating a man to death who had gotten angry because they threw an egg at him, and of the ongoing slaughter—and slaughters to come—in the Middle East.

Violence lies in the heart of all that exists on this planet: in lobsters and minuscule octopuses stalking the ocean's depths, in thousand-legged bugs crawling in the dirt, in mothers escorting their preschool daughters across parking lots.

Mayhem is woven into the soul of our universe, no matter how peaceful our surroundings might appear at any given moment.

The old Christians used to call this concept, this idea that all earthy creatures are tainted by a propensity toward destruction, "original sin." You don't hear much about original sin anymore. But it's still with us every day, everywhere. Even in our paradises.

NO QUESTION TOO COSMIC
FOR RELIGION GURU

November 30, 2002

It's high time for an installment of "Ask the Religion Guru," in which your discerning correspondent, being almost omniscient, tackles some of the cosmic questions about which his readers wonder:

Dear Religion Guru: This issue has troubled me since my parochial school days. How many angels can dance on the head of a pin? Thanks. —Faithful in Florence

Dear Faithful: Good question. Theologians and mystics who have wrestled on the horns of this dilemma—and suffered grievous wounds in the process—include St. Augustine the Hippo and my second cousin, the Apostle Nimrod "Tater" Chestnut of the Living Word of Prophetic Holiness Bible Believing Fire Baptized Church and Tabernacle of Foot Washing Splendor in His Mighty Name Amen.

The correct answer is 5.7256 angels. Glad the Religion Guru could clear that up.

Dear Religion Guru: How many angels can dance on a diamond? Thanks. —Worldly in Wolfe County

Dear Worldly: Good question. The answer is nine—if they're Anaheim Angels. Hahaha. Oh, the Religion Guru is so witty he can barely stand himself.

Dear Religion Guru: I understand you personally have met His Holiness the Dalai Lama. When greeting the Dalai Lama, what is the proper form of address? Thanks. —Baffled in Berea

Dear Baffled: Good question. Actually, and I say this with all humility, His Holiness met the Religion Guru. But we won't quibble.

The correct form of address is, "Hello, Dalai."

Dear Religion Guru: What is the one true faith? Thanks.   —Seeker in Somerset

Dear Seeker: Good question. The Religion Guru defers on this point to the wonderful Appalachian scholar Loyal Jones, who has written somewhere (the Religion Guru, even though he's nearly omniscient, can't remember where and doesn't care to look it up) that the true religion is the Baptist faith.

Every other belief system is an offshoot of that one. For instance, Methodists are Baptists who are scared of water. Presbyterians are Baptists who have been to college. Episcopalians are Baptists whose deals worked out.

The Religion Guru might add that Pentecostals are Baptists who are multilingual.

Dear Religion Guru: What is the coolest name for a Christian rock band you have ever heard? Thanks.   —Boogieing in Beattyville

Dear Boogieing: Good question. Some years ago the Religion Guru attended a concert by a local band called Fling Down Jezebel. That was a very cool name. Indeed, the name was better than the music.

Dear Religion Guru: If you possessed musical talent and could form your own Christian band, what would you call it?   Thanks.
—Holy Rocker in Hell-for-Certain

Dear Holy: Good question. The Religion Guru would call his band Elisha's Hairpiece. There's this Old Testament story about the prophet who was sensitive about his baldness. When a crew of younger—and presumably hirsute—men made fun of his shiny dome, Elisha sicced bears on them. Several dozen of the scoffers were eaten alive.

The older the Religion Guru gets, the more he appreciates that story.

Dear Religion Guru: Did you forget you had a column due this week and then knock out this one in a hurried, not to mention feeble, attempt to rip off Dave Barry's "Ask Mr. Language Person"?
—Nobody's Fool in Fleming-Neon

Dear Fool: Bad question. Do the words "Elisha" and "bears" mean anything to you, smart aleck?

ABSENCE CAN MAKE
THE FAITHFUL STRONGER

December 21, 2002

I've rediscovered the uncomfortable fact that, as a pastor, I'm nearly irrelevant. It was another slap to my ego, but it will prove in the long haul to have been a blessing to me as well as to others, I trust.

The lesson happened like this. After two and a half years of taking care of my ill wife, I departed in September for a desperately needed sabbatical. Renee stayed with her folks.

My congregation granted me an extended vacation from my church duties. A committee comprised almost entirely of laypeople ran the joint while I was away.

I traveled from sea to shining sea, from Maine to California. Finally I spent a few weeks at home alternately reading, watching TV and playing the stereo very loud.

I didn't worry much about Renee. I checked on her daily, but I knew her parents would lovingly tend to her.

I was more concerned about the church. I wondered how the members would fare without me, whether they would drift away in apathy or start bickering.

The good news is, I returned last month to find the congregation running perfectly. Everybody was in good spirits and cooperating well. The committee had brought in a series of accomplished guest speakers. The finances were solid. Attendance was at an all-time high.

The bad news is, the place was running terrifically, and nobody was fussing. The guest speakers were, by all accounts, great. The finances were strong. Attendance was up.

I mentioned this to a pal.

"Yeah," he said. "Remind me again what we pay you for."

24

After some soul-searching, I decided that maybe this is how a healthy church actually ought to function. Maybe ministers ought to try to make themselves invisible.

I draw inspiration here from no less an example than Jesus.

According to my religion's lore, at age thirty-three, Jesus reached the apex of his spiritual power. He snatched the keys to hell from Satan, broke out of his own tomb and returned resurrected from the dead, permeated with glory and surrounded by angels.

If this is true, then obviously he could have ruled not only the church but the planet. You know what he did instead?

He left. He disappeared—and turned over the day-to-day decisions to his disciples, a bunch of knotheads if ever knotheads existed.

He said it was to their advantage that he go.

I think he meant that as long as he stuck around to do everything for them, they would never be forced to depend on themselves, or on God, for anything.

But Jesus wanted them to mature, to make mistakes, to deepen their faith. So he told them, "Hey, I'm outta here. You boys call if you need me."

Maybe he also realized that as long as he remained where he was, confined to his own two legs, he could accomplish the work of only one man. But if he delegated the labor to twelve guys—yahoos, yes, but faithful yahoos—they'd eventually do twelve times more than he could. The results would multiply.

Instead of one leader there would be a dozen, then eventually 100, then 1,000.

OK, clearly I'm not Jesus (as if you were confused about that).

And I left my congregation for a briefer period and for a different reason. The people on the committee who took my place are no more knuckleheaded than I am.

Still, I found this same truth in my church: To the extent that I stepped aside, others stepped up. The committee members seemed to get more work accomplished than I usually do, and at the same time, their own faith grew.

But it's a hard lesson to learn, this idea of leading more effectively by doing less. As typical humans, we ministers like to think we're the centers of our churches' shows.

We're not. God is. Sometimes we block his spotlight.

WHAT WOULD JESUS SAY
ABOUT WHAT WE DO?

January 18, 2003

For once, I was way ahead of a trend rather than way behind it. Which only proves—to steal a line from a Knott County friend—that even a blind squirrel gets a hickory nut once in a while.

You've heard, no doubt, about the "What Would Jesus Drive?" ad campaign launched by the Pennsylvania-based Evangelical Environmental Network. The group's aim is to discourage Christians from buying gas-hog, sport utility vehicles.

Of course, the "What Would Jesus Drive?" ads clearly are a takeoff on the "What Would Jesus Do?" movement, which was popular a few years ago.

Well, we actually anticipated all this right here in the *Herald-Leader* way back in 1991, before either question made headlines nationwide.

I wrote an opus then called "If Jesus Came to Lexington," in which I asked various religious leaders and laypeople what would happen if the Jesus portrayed in the New Testament were to suddenly show up in Kentucky.

Where would he work? How would he dress? Where would he worship?

And yes—what would he drive? (The answers to that one included a Jeep, an '86 Nova and the speculation that Jesus would prefer to hitchhike.)

OK, let me come clean. If you must know, I wasn't even ahead of that trend. I was about a century behind it.

27

In the 1890s, the Rev. Charles M. Sheldon wrote a novel, *In His Steps*, about the residents of a Kansas town who begin behaving exactly as they think Jesus would if he were in their shoes. Within forty years of its first publication, *In His Steps* had sold 22 million copies. Apparently, Jesus would write a mega-best seller.

Anyway, the point is—and yes, there is a point—for a dozen years I've noticed a curious phenomenon in how these questions tend to be answered: Nearly all the people you ask seem to think Jesus is very much like them.

The environmentally conscious Evangelical Environmental Network says Jesus would drive a Toyota Prius, which has a hybrid gasoline-electric motor.

That's fine with me. I drive an SUV myself, but buying it was my wife's idea. (Or, as Adam wailed in the Garden, it was the woman the Lord gave me who caused me to sin.) I couldn't care less what I drive as long as it has a good stereo.

But because I don't care what I drive, I don't think Jesus would care, either.

Seriously, when I recently reread my 1991 story, here's what I found.

I asked people to describe Jesus if he showed up in contemporary Lexington.

My old buddy, Rabbi Jon Adland, said Jesus would be "a liberal, social activist Jew." Adland himself is a liberal, social activist Jew.

But a Catholic scholar said Jesus would be an ecumenical Roman Catholic.

The Rev. Kelly Flood, then minister of Lexington's Unitarian Universalist Church—known for its early acceptance of women's and gay rights—thought Jesus might arrive as a woman and would embrace gay people particularly.

A black Methodist layman said Jesus would be black and male.

I asked what Jesus' occupation would be.

The late Jerry Hammond said Jesus would be a carpenter again: "I see no reason to expect that he would have changed occupations. That's an honorable one, one of the more useful occupations that we've ever developed."

True enough, but it's interesting that Hammond was a leader of Kentucky's building and construction unions.

Do we detect a pattern yet?

On one hand, it's probably good that we each find in Jesus someone with whom we can identify—a Jesus who is so all-encompassing that he actually becomes, in a sense, each of us, no matter our denomination, our race, our job. That says there's something about him for everybody, and something about everybody that would please him.

On the other hand, we also manipulate our interpretations of Jesus and his teachings to suit our agendas. We remake him in our image, instead of vice versa. That's natural, perhaps, but it's not good.

We do both these things at the same time, and it's hard to tell where one leaves off and the other begins—when we're truly seeing, in some small way, a presence of the real Jesus in ourselves, and when we're merely co-opting him to justify our own pursuits.

IF YOU NEED HELP,
DON'T SHRINK FROM GETTING IT

February 15, 2003

Most people I hang out with are Christians who seem fairly serious about their faith.

Recently it occurred to me that about half of these same people are, on a regular basis, seeing psychiatrists, psychologists or marriage counselors. And they're taking one of a cornucopia of antidepressant drugs just so they can navigate their daily lives without killing themselves or anyone else.

Depression, disillusionment and despair seem to be the norm, even in the church.

For years, there's been a quiet but monumental shift in the ways religious people deal with these mental health issues: Millions have decided to avail themselves of whatever psychiatric or pharmaceutical aid is legally available.

You hear parishioners debating the merits of Paxil versus Prozac with the sort of fervor they used to reserve for arguments about whether Romans was a better book of the Bible than Revelation.

Meanwhile, in my experience, the other half of churchgoers tend to bad-mouth the ones seeking professional help. This contrarian view holds that real Christians don't need therapy, that psychology is paganism disguised with a Ph.D., and that antidepressants are Satan's own opiate for the masses.

Certainly there was a time and place—my boyhood in rural Kentucky churches—when if you saw a shrink, much less took nerve pills, you were considered crazy. You also were considered a weak Christian;

30

you obviously didn't have enough spiritual spine to depend on the Lord and walk in joy.

Well, you know what I say?

Those days should be past. Hooray for the head shrinkers.

Sure, their use can be abused. And I don't think they're any real substitute for God's tangible presence in our lives; that's about the only thing that ever brings us a measure of true peace.

But the problem is, God often tends to make himself notably scarce. That apparently is part of his plan. The theological experts tell me it's how he forges our character, by disappearing occasionally and forcing us to fight for faith.

Maybe you've experienced this. When everything's going well—your marriage is euphoric, you've won a big promotion, your kid gets accepted to Yale—you can practically hear God's audible voice at every turn. He's offering you a cigar.

Find out your husband's having an affair, get canned from your job or see your child sent to rehab with a cocaine addiction, and that's when God decides to take a vacation. He leaves for Norway and forgets his cell phone.

I advise that in those times you get all the professional intervention you can afford. After all, depression and loneliness are nothing new. It's not as if God is shocked by our inability to cope. Here's a quote that's a few thousand years old:

"My tears have been my food day and night.... I pour out my soul.... O my God, my soul is in despair within me."

Or try this one:

"Awake, O Lord! Why do you sleep? Rouse yourself!... Why do you hide your face and forget our misery and oppression? We are brought down to dust; our bodies cling to the ground."

Both of those are from King David. Maybe the psalmist could have benefited from a few counseling sessions, you know? Crawl up out of that dust, David.

All of God's people—and all the devil's people too, I suppose—have bad days. And bad years. And sometimes bad decades.

That's the way it's always been. The difference now is that other humans can alleviate some of the suffering.

If you had a headache, you'd take an aspirin, right? If you're depressed, pray. And then pop a few Prozac. (With your doctor's guidance.)

Maybe God will show up tomorrow and miraculously deliver you. But until he does, it's OK—even advisable—to take any safe port in a storm.

And if you're not having trouble coping, praise the Lord and quit passing judgment. Because tomorrow might be your day. You're not as strong as you think.

HUMBLE LIVES CAN YIELD
GREAT SIGNIFICANCE

March 29, 2003

L ast week my son, John, and I took a driving tour of the South. I noticed something I've noticed before, but which never ceases to fascinate me: The most extraordinary events often occur in the most ordinary of places. Similarly the most ordinary-appearing people sometimes perform history-making acts.

For instance, in downtown Memphis, John and I toured the National Civil Rights Museum at the site of the Lorraine Motel.

The motel's sign and a few of its rooms remain much as they were on April 4, 1968, when Martin Luther King, Jr., was assassinated on the Lorraine's balcony. Room 306 still has room service coffee cups sitting out on trays. The beds are unmade.

Across a courtyard, the Young/Morrow Boarding house, from which James Earl Ray allegedly fired the infamous shot, has been turned into a section of the museum. The tiny room Ray rented, as well as the communal bathroom from which he apparently aimed his rifle, have been faithfully re-created from police photos.

Certainly, few events in the 20th century had greater repercussions than the killing of King that spring afternoon.

But what struck me as I walked the site was the humility—you might even say, seediness—of the scene: the motel's tacky greenish-blue doors, the stripped-down decor of the Lorraine's rooms, the grimy bathtub and peeling wallpaper in Ray's boardinghouse. When Ray was arrested, he had a snub-nosed .38 revolver. It's on display in the museum; the pistol-butt's grips are held together with black electrical tape.

33

I don't know what I'd expected. But it startled me that King, a No-bel Peace Prize winner, the father of the civil rights movement, could have been gunned down in so wretched a place, by such a wretchedly ordinary criminal.

Next, John and I stopped at Sun Studio, where popular music and Western culture were forever transformed.

Owner Sam Phillips recorded the first rock 'n' roll song there: It was called "Rocket 88," and featured on piano a then-obscure Ike Turner. Later, a local truck driver named Elvis walked in off the street and started cutting records. Jerry Lee Lewis, Carl Perkins, Roy Orbison and Johnny Cash soon followed him.

The building is an old storefront. Its outer bricks are weather-worn.

Phillips laid the original tan tiles that remain on the floor inside the studio and the acoustical tiles on its walls and ceiling. An "X" of, again, black tape marks the spot where Elvis stood to belt out his earliest hits. You can stand on the "X" and, if you're brave enough, sing into the very microphone he sang into.

The studio itself is about the size of my den. The rows of acoustical tiles are crooked—Phillips may have been a musical genius, but as a carpenter he was an amateur.

Another day, John and I visited Oxford, Miss. We found Rowan Oak, the home of the late William Faulkner, who won the Nobel Prize for literature and may have been the only American writer you could favorably compare with, say, Shakespeare.

Faulkner's clapboard house was large but run-down, shrouded in shadows that made it appear appropriately gothic. The paint was peeling. John and I wandered the grounds undisturbed, for a while the only people there. John sat on Faulkner's porch.

The day after that we headed for Tupelo, to see the two-room shot-gun shack where Elvis was born. As I recall, Elvis' father built the place for $180. The family had to move later because Vernon Presley couldn't make the payments.

I've often thought that if we could journey back in time we would be astounded, and a bit disheartened, by how unremarkable our religious heroes appeared in their day, too. I wonder whether you or I would have taken a second notice of Abraham or Jesus.

I wonder what mighty works the ordinary people around us are doing today: our next-door neighbor, the guitar player in the pub, the nursing home worker.

I wonder whether we ever recognize geniuses or saints except in hindsight.

MOM WAS AN ANGEL
TO ALL WHO KNEW HER

May 31, 2003

Her death didn't attract any media interest. CNN ignored it. The Herald-Leader gave her a couple of perfunctory sentences among the daily obituaries.

But on May 7, the only genuine saint I ever met went to her reward. Her name was Alice Chestnut Prather, she was sixty-nine, and she was my mother.

I don't remember ever having been angry with her. There was no reason to be: In my whole life, she never did me anything but good.

By choice, my mom stayed in the background. If she had any particular ambitions, I'm not aware of them. She didn't finish college, wasn't active in social clubs.

For fifty years, she served as the wife of a minister, quietly helping organize potluck dinners and teaching Sunday school classes. For twenty-two of those years, she also worked as a secretary for the Montgomery County school system. When she died, she was retired.

Yet the outpouring of affection and grief at her funeral-home visitation topped anything I've ever witnessed.

Several times, teary-eyed mourners of various ages took me off to the side and said things such as this: "Alice was more of a mom to me than my own mother was. Whenever I had a problem I'd go talk to her. She'd listen for hours. She never judged me. She never seemed shocked. Oh, I loved that woman so much."

My mom had never mentioned these counseling sessions to me.

Our local high school has a terrific choral program. At the funeral home, the choir director told me my mother was a main reason the program exists. He had paid tribute to her that day in his classes. When he was a new teacher, she encouraged him, coached him and recruited singers for him, he said. He couldn't have lasted without her, he said.

I never had a clue.

My mom didn't have a martyr's complex. She simply cared about people—the great and the outcast—and did what she could to make their lot easier.

Earlier this year, she was diagnosed with cancer. Hers turned out to be an unusually aggressive malignancy.

On the last evening of April, her back hurt and she could hardly breathe. We took her to the emergency room.

A doctor there showed her and me an X-ray of tumors speckling her lungs. Mom didn't appear frightened. She looked at me and said, "Now don't you get down-hearted. I'm not dead yet, so don't start my funeral. God's still in control."

She was more concerned about me than about herself.

By the next day, the prognosis was grimmer. She might have only days or even hours left. The news spread.

Our family is small. But that night people spontaneously poured into the hospital from every direction. They filled my mom's room and lined two corridors. Hospital workers tried to shoo them away, but they wouldn't budge.

At 2 a.m., Mom's room was packed with teen-agers, only two of whom were kin to us. They sat and stood in a semi-circle around her, adjusting electric fans so she could get some cool air, patting her legs, offering her sips of water, joking with her.

You see, my mom and dad had raised my nephew Will. Before my mom got sick, Will and his buddies often rolled into my parents' home at midnight, starving, as young men always are. No matter the hour, my mom would happily fix them stacks of grilled cheese sandwiches, bake batches of homemade cookies, whatever they wanted. It seemed that half the kids in town called her "Grandma Alice."

Now that she was sick, these same muscular guys stood guard over her. She drifted off to sleep, then woke up and wanted to know what had happened while she was out. The boys told her they'd given her a tattoo on her rump: "G-Maw."

She grinned.

She asked what time it was. A young man said, "It's time for you to get up and bake cookies, Grandma."

A week later, at her funeral, these fellows wept openly. The next Sunday, several came to our church and sat down front in her honor.

There's much more I'd like to say and too little space in which to do my mother justice. The bottom line is this: She loved God. As a result she loved people, and accepted them, and did what she could to help them—which for her mainly meant fixing them sandwiches or listening to their troubles.

In performing those humble acts, she probably had a greater impact on the lives of more people than any ten preachers I could name. I am so grateful to have been her son. I miss her so badly.

WHEN TO FORGIVE AND WHEN TO FIGHT

July 19, 2003

A friend asked me this intriguing question: Are Christians required to be doormats?

The answer's not simple. Starting with the Bible, and across 2,000 years of church history, there's been an ongoing tension on this subject. One side says Christians shouldn't fight back even when we're wronged, that we should be as self-sacrificing as Jesus.

The other side says we have a duty to confront evil, that occasionally we must literally or metaphorically punch bullies in their noses. (I'm addressing the Christian tradition because I know more about my religion's strengths, contradictions and foibles than I do about Buddhism or Islam.)

Even the New Testament appears to contradict itself.

Jesus teaches that we should be, essentially, pacifists: If an angry person slaps us on one cheek, we're to turn the other cheek. If a bad guy demands our shirt, we're to offer up our coat, too. If our enemy is hungry, we're to feed her. You know the drill.

But other biblical passages, such as the writings of St. Paul, suggest limits to this meekness. We're told that if a man won't work, we're to let him starve. We're told that governments are ordained by God to wield a sword against evildoers.

So, how do we find a balance between endless mercy and appropriate confrontation? Here are principles I think will help us decide when we should turn the other cheek and when, so to speak, we should kick some posterior (in love, of course):

• It's never our place to repay evil on our own. We're not justified in whacking our neighbor with a ball-peen hammer, except in direct self-defense, perhaps. We often need cooler heads to help us decide what's wrong and right in our conflicts with other people. That's why God ordains church elders. That's why we have juries.

• When we find ourselves in conflict with another person, even as we're wounded or angry, we should seek the good of our adversary. There's a simple reason Jesus commanded us to pray for our enemies: If God converts an enemy and softens her heart and pricks her conscience, she won't be our enemy anymore. She'll be a friend.

• Still, seeking the good of others also means considering those likely to be hurt by this enemy. If, to cite an extreme example, you're attacked by a serial rapist, he might insist that you show him mercy by not pressing charges—but if you don't prosecute, you're endangering innocent people the rapist will attack tomorrow.

• Any time we have a problem with another person, we need to look truthfully and humbly at our own failings in the matter. We need to consider how we contributed to the argument. We need to ask ourselves what we might do differently.

• In day-to-day disagreements (I'm talking about personality conflicts here, not serial rape), we should try to restore the damaged relationship privately. That is, we don't tell Uncle Luther or Aunt Sudie how badly we were treated. We go to our adversary and gently attempt to work out the issue between us.

• If that attempt fails, however, we then present the problem to a few impartial mediators. If it's a problem between us and another Christian, we discuss it with the pastor or elders. The hope is that, once again, the dispute can be solved quietly, that hurt feelings can be mended. We want to see whether we're mistaken as much as we want to see our adversary's mistakes pointed out to him.

• If the disagreement still can't be fixed, we may be forced to take the issue before the entire church or, in secular matters, to court.

• Occasionally, very occasionally, for the sake of peace, we have to quit hanging around certain people. The kindest route might be to love somebody from a distance: We move on to another church; we file for divorce; we dissolve a business partnership. But this is the last resort, when nothing else has worked. Our goal should be restoration, whenever that's possible.

God recognizes we're flawed humans living on a flawed planet among other flawed people. Ideally, as Christians, we should be able to solve most disputes through charity, forgiveness and compromise. Sadly, it's not an ideal world. We need to turn the other cheek, but we don't have to let people stomp our guts out over and over.

THE FAMILY DOESN'T FARE WELL
IN SCRIPTURE

October 18, 2003

For two decades I've taught my fellow churchgoers about the Bible. To this day, I don't consider myself an expert on that marvelous, and marvelously complex, book, but I am familiar with it.

Sometimes when I hear TV preachers or politicians use the Judeo-Christian Scriptures as the justification for their cause—whether they're liberals or conservatives, whether they're railing against the war in Iraq or trying to post the ten Commandments in courthouses—I feel as if they must be reading some different Bible than I am.

Conservatives, for instance, frequently have cited the Old and New Testaments as the basis for their beliefs in "family values."

I'm quite sympathetic to most of those values. I've been married to one woman for twenty-five years. I'm a devoted father. My own parents were happily married for five decades. I get along well with my sister, which can be a feat in itself.

Yet, as I've told my congregation, if you're seeking examples of how to maintain a healthy family, the Bible is about the last place you ought to look.

The Bible is, from beginning to end, essentially a litany of every imaginable family dysfunction. The trend starts in Genesis with Adam and Eve, whose son Cain murders his brother, Abel.

There's Noah who, after surviving the flood, drinks himself into a stupor. While Noah is passed out, one of his sons apparently commits, or at least contemplates, some incestuous deed with his dad—the details are ambiguous.

42

Then we encounter Abraham, the great patriarch of faith. While married to Sarah, he sires a son with Sarah's maid. Abraham also twice gives Sarah to other men.

Abraham's nephew Lot gets his daughters pregnant—while he's drunk. Abraham's sons Isaac and Ishmael despise each other.

Next, Isaac's younger son, Jacob, steals his brother Esau's inheritance by deceiving their dad, abetted in this con job by the boys' mother.

In the following generation, several of Jacob's sons sell their brother Joseph to slave traders, then cover up their crime by faking his death.

And we're still in Genesis. We're not even out of the opening book!

Move on, and you'll discover that Moses has a terrible time with his sister and brother, who are critical of his leadership and think him a hypocrite.

Among Jesus' direct ancestors is Rahab, the hooker.

King David has an adulterous affair with a neighbor and orders her husband killed. One of David's sons rapes his own sister. Another son murders the rapist brother and eventually is slain while leading a revolution against David.

David's son Solomon takes several hundred wives and concubines—think of him as an Israelite Wilt Chamberlain—and starts worshiping pagan idols to placate his harem.

Then there's Samson. He has a fetish for foreign prostitutes. Any time he happens not to get his way with them, he goes berserk and slaughters anyone unfortunate enough to be nearby.

New Testament figures fare a little better in the family values department, but only a little.

Jesus, of course, never marries at all or has biological children. His siblings are openly hostile toward him, and he disses them in return. His extended family believes he's insane, and says so. This all is recorded plainly in the Gospels.

St. Paul stays single during his public ministry. Even one of Paul's conservative modern biographers has argued that Paul probably was divorced.

So, on one hand, the Bible in its didactic passages does tell us that we should abstain from sexual relations before marriage; that after we're married we should remain faithful to our spouse; that we should serve our children and our parents devotedly; that we should keep the peace with our brothers and sisters.

On the other hand, it offers us hardly any tales of actual human beings who managed to do all these things. I find the Bible fascinating partly because, in my estimation, it's so relentlessly candid. It spares its heroes no more than its villains. They're three-dimensional, self-contradictory. Just like people today.

But that being the case, the real Bible also doesn't lend itself very well to polarizing political movements of the left or right. Or shouldn't.

Instead, it admonishes us sinners about what we ought to do, but shows us again and again why we probably won't. And it tells us that God manages to love us anyhow.

A MESSAGE FROM GOD
AT A LIQUOR STORE

December 20, 2003

My niece Chrystin is a bright and beautiful young woman. She plans to earn a master's degree in social work and eventually a Ph.D. in clinical psychology. Plus, she's a dead ringer for actress Halle Berry.

Shortly after she received her bachelor's degree, Chrystin, twenty-three, was offered a job in Cincinnati working as a therapist to groups of troubled children. The pay was great, and the job would give her hands-on clinical experience, so she decided to postpone graduate school. A lifelong churchgoer, she believed God had opened up this opportunity for her.

Once she'd relocated, Chrystin discovered the job wasn't as ideal as she'd thought it would be. The children with whom she was working were more troubled than she'd anticipated. They required strong medication, which they sometimes refused to take. Several were violent. Chrystin found herself breaking up fistfights. She was assaulted. Worse, her supervisors were so stressed that they weren't much easier to deal with than the kids.

Chrystin worried whether she'd made the right decision in moving away from her family and putting off graduate school. She wondered whether she should quit her job.

Her professional problems started carrying over into other areas of her life.

One day after, work she was an emotional shambles. She headed for her boyfriend's house. His mother was cooking dinner for them.

Chrystin arrived in a foul disposition. She didn't like any of the food. While the others ate, Chrystin went off to sit alone in the den. After dinner, she and her boyfriend got into an argument. Chrystin realized the spat was her fault. She was so wrung out that nothing anyone could do was going to please her.

"I'm leaving," she told her boyfriend. "I'm going to stop and get some beer, go home and drink it, and then go to sleep."

She drove toward the home she shares with her stepsister and her stepsister's husband. On the way, she saw a liquor store, veered into the parking lot and pulled up to the drive-through window. A woman she'd never met opened the glass.

"Give me a six-pack of Miller Lite," Chrystin said.

The woman walked away. She returned without the six-pack.

"Honey," the woman said, "your job is going to be just fine. Don't you worry. God's got a plan for you. You're in the right place. Don't doubt yourself."

Chrystin stared at her, dumfounded.

"Do you go to church?" the woman said. "Do you go to a charismatic church?"

Chrystin laughed. "Well, yeah. I mean, I was raised in that kind of church. I moved up here a few months ago and I haven't been to church anywhere recently."

The woman explained that when she'd started for the cooler to fetch Chrystin's beer, God had told her to give Chrystin a message from him instead: "The Lord said, 'Speak to her and tell her everything's going to be fine.'"

The woman went on to say that she and her husband owned the liquor store and that she attended a non-denominational church where the gifts of the Holy Spirit—including personal prophecies—operated freely.

"Do you still want the beer?" the lady said.

"You can keep it," Chrystin said.

And drove away.

She told me this story a few days later on the phone. Her faith had been rejuvenated.

"Everything she was saying was just hitting me right in the heart," Chrystin said of the woman. "It was so clear. It basically just lifted, like a load off my shoulders."

Chrystin was at peace again. Her job seemed brand-new. She knew she could help those troubled kids after all. She was where the Lord intended her to be.

"It was just the best thing I could have heard," she said.

OK, drinking a few beers isn't a mortal sin, but it's not an appropriate way to manage stress, either. And, let's face it, if you need to receive a word from God, you don't usually head to a liquor store to find it.

That's what I love about this story. If you believe Chrystin's tale, and I do, the Lord seems to have taken her problems—and her questionable decision about how to deal with them—and turned the whole situation for good. Chrystin found that even when she was in the pits, God was watching out for her.

Apparently he guided her to a specific drive-up window—and met her there.

He didn't rebuke her for her lack of faith or her fondness for Miller Lite (and, for that matter, neither did he condemn the Christian lady who ran liquor the store).

Instead he chose to bless Chrystin.

Therein lies a lesson for all of us, Christians and non-Christians, beer guzzlers and teetotalers alike.

CAREGIVERS COULD USE HELP
OF THEIR OWN

July 17, 2004

More than four years ago, my wife, Renee, was diagnosed with advanced cancer and given only a few months to live. Remarkably, she's still here, still plugging along.

She's also still desperately ill, a hospice patient, confined to a recliner in our den, unable to tend to many of her routine physical needs. I'm her primary caregiver.

If nothing else, our experience has focused my attention on the vast number of people who, like me, spend much of their time and all of their energy caring for disabled loved ones. Before, I'd never much noticed caregivers. Today, I see them everywhere—wives nursing husbands through the horrors of Lou Gehrig's disease, mothers caring for quadriplegic teenagers, adult children looking after parents who suffer from Alzheimer's.

I've discovered that when a person is afflicted with a long-term illness, the one closest to him suffers as much as the patient does (and in some cases more, experts say).

Yet, caregivers often are ignored, and occasionally misunderstood, by church workers, family, friends and sometimes even by medical professionals.

For a slew of reasons, caregiving might be the world's hardest job.

It's hard not because you don't love the patient you're taking care of. It's hard because you do. Watching a spouse or child suffer month after month, year after year, takes a profound toll.

It's common for ill people to become angry and vindictive as they battle their illnesses. It's also common for them to turn those searing

48

emotions against the one nearest them: the family member trying hardest to help. It's difficult enough to nurse a disabled person; it's twenty times harder when that person blames you for his pain.

Here are a few of the numerous other pressures that caregivers routinely face:

- Financial problems. Perhaps the sick person was the family's primary breadwinner but can no longer work. Sometimes it's difficult for the caregiver to hold down a job while tending a disabled spouse. Then there are all those medical bills.

- Role changes. A man whose wife is on a ventilator might have to become mother as well as father to their children. Adults caring for elderly parents can find themselves forced to act as parent to their moms or dads.

- Confinement. Caregivers are trapped at home for days or weeks at a stretch. They'd love to take a vacation, go to the movies or simply drive to the grocery. They feel as if they're under house arrest.

- Loss of physical affection. An ill spouse might be too sick to have sex—or even to rub his wife's neck. Yet the caregiver still needs a normal physical relationship. (Some wag said sex is like air: It's not that important until you're not getting any.)

- Loneliness. The caregiver often feels robbed of work, friends, church. He or she might not be able to talk freely to the sick person, for any number of reasons.

- Loss of faith. Many caregivers struggle to maintain their previous trust in a loving God, as they witness a level of suffering they're never encountered before.

- Guilt. Frequently they feel guilty because they can't do more to help their loved ones, or because they are themselves healthy, or because, on bad days, they'd rather see their love ones die than live in their present conditions.

- Dread. A caregiver worries about what he or she will do if the sick person does die. They wonder who will take care of them if they become ill, too.

- Total burnout. See all of the above.

Despite all that, caregivers typically suffer in silence. They don't feel free to express their own pain, when someone they love is suffering so more visibly. They're afraid their friends will think they're selfish. Consequently they turn their agony inward.

A mental-health counselor told me that, over time, a disproportionate number of caregivers find themselves drawn to self-destructive behaviors. They abuse alcohol; they have extramarital affairs; they desert their ill loved ones and disappear; or they develop serious health problems of their own, such as depression, hypertension or heart trouble.

There's quite a bit you can do to help them.

First, never, ever, judge. You might think you know how you'd react if your husband, mom or child were ill—but trust me, you don't. Not until you've been there.

Second, give the caregiver a safe—by which I mean both a non-judgmental and confidential—place to vent. Just listen. And listen.

Third, volunteer to sit with the sick person for a day so the caregiver can get out. Better, hire someone else to sit with the sick person and take the caregiver out yourself.

Fourth, insist that the caregiver nurture his or her own health.

Fifth, pray for all concerned.

CAREGIVERS AREN'T PERFECT;
WE'RE HUMAN

July 31, 2004

My last column, about the emotional, spiritual and financial trials of being a full-time caregiver to a disabled loved one, drew an unusually large volume of responses.

The vast majority of people I heard from were other caregivers, almost all of whom said, in essence, "I thought I was the only one struggling to cope."

Knowing now that I have a ready-made and sympathetic audience on this subject, I want to add a few more observations, based partly on my own experiences and research and partly on the insights of readers.

There are 44.4 million people in the United States who provide unpaid care for other adults, according to a survey by the MetLife Foundation for the National Alliance for Caregiving and AARP.

- Eighty-three percent of these people tend sick relatives.
- Nearly six in ten caregivers have worked other jobs while providing care.
- About four in ten caregivers are men.
- The average length of caregiving is 4.3 years. But among caregivers fifty to sixty-four years old, seventeen percent have provided care for more than a decade. (You think you've got it hard!)
- One survey finds that prayer is caregivers' most effective means of dealing with their situations. Nearly three in four caregivers say prayer helps them. Two-thirds say it's also helpful to talk with friends or relatives about their difficulties.

Experts describe five levels of intensity in caregiving. Someone on Level 1 might simply need to drive an aging parent to the doctor or the grocery a few times a week. Level 5 caregivers provide constant care to desperately sick people who can't do much of anything for themselves.

Caregivers at the lower levels often find the experience rewarding. As the level rises, so does the toll. Among Level 5 caregivers, about a third suffer physical or mental problems themselves because of stress.

The mail I've received suggests it's even harder to take care of a loved one who's suffering from a mental impairment, such as a brain injury or Alzheimer's, than one who's suffering from cancer or heart disease. A reader tells me that eighty percent of marriages in which a spouse has suffered a brain injury end in divorce.

I'd long assumed that for whatever reasons—cultural, biological or some combination—women generally handle the demands of caregiving better than men do. If my correspondents are a representative sample, that stereotype is wrong.

For every man who wrote, I heard from eight or ten women, and apparently they're every bit as frustrated, lonely, angry and scared as the men. Maybe they just hide their feelings better. One woman summed it up best. She said she suffers head and neck pain from wearing such a brave face.

Last time, I listed personal struggles that caregivers often contend with. I omitted a biggie: anger. Caregivers get angry at the sick person for putting them in this spot; they get angry at themselves for not being more saintly; they get angry at relatives for not pulling their share; they get angry at God for not intervening.

Several caregivers asked me whether I thought professional counseling would be appropriate for them. Here's my philosophy, folks: Grab whatever works, as long as it's not more destructive than what you're already dealing with.

If you think talking to a shrink will help, have at it. If you need Prozac, get it. If you think running a marathon will lift your spirits, start training today. If your neighbors or family don't understand that, too bad. You gotta do what you gotta do, to keep doing what you're doing.

It's tough—unimaginably tough—to be critically ill. But it's also tough to take care of someone else who's ill.

If you're trying to do that and you don't feel swell about it every waking moment, don't condemn yourself. It doesn't mean you're evil. It means you're human. You're not perfect, but neither is anyone else. Hang in there. Give it your best shot.

And God bless you.

SEARCH FOR TRUTH BEGINS
WITH HEART

August 21, 2004

At a stoplight the other day, I noticed this bumper sticker on the car in front of me: "Big Bang Theory: God spoke and BANG! It happened."

Because I'm a nerd, that sticker started me thinking again about one of the more controversial questions in modern Christianity. How much of the Bible—and specifically in this case, the Genesis story of creation—is literally true and how much is myth or metaphor? Congregations and whole denominations have ruptured over that issue.

On one side, you have those who insist the Genesis account, and other Bible stories, are factually correct down to the least detail, that God made the Earth in six twenty-four-hour days, that Adam and Eve were two specific people. If we can't believe the Bible when it tells us those things, they argue, then we can't believe anything else it says.

At the other pole are those of a scientific bent, who assume the world is closed to supernatural intervention, that it evolved slowly and accidentally after a cosmic explosion.

My opinion, for what it's worth, is that the whole argument misses the point.

When, as a young adult, I first began seeking spiritual enlightenment (having spent my formative years as a wastrel), a friend loaned me a copy of Flannery O'Connor's *The Complete Stories*. O'Connor ranks among the great literary masters of the 20th century. She also was a devoted Christian. Her stories opened up faith to me as nothing before had. Their cumulative effect was about like getting smacked upside the head with a two-by-four, spiritually speaking.

54

Among the better-known pieces in that collection is "A Good Man Is Hard to Find." In it, a Southern family sets off on vacation driving toward Florida, against the shrill protests of the family's self-centered grandmother, who wants them all to visit relatives in Tennessee. Along the road they encounter an escaped sociopath called The Misfit. He and his gang murder the whole family.

The grandmother is the last to be killed. Just before she dies, she has a religious revelation. She touches The Misfit in a gesture of godly love. The Misfit fires three shots into her chest.

"She would of been a good woman," he says afterward, "if it had been somebody there to shoot her every minute of her life."

I'm not aware of a more profound statement about the human condition. Most of us tend to be smug and petty. Usually, only cataclysmic moments of weakness—our own impending death, say—can force us to see ourselves for what we truly are, to acknowledge our need for God's help and to reach out compassionately toward others.

But O'Connor's stories aren't "true" in the strict sense; they're not factual. This grandmother never actually existed. She wasn't murdered by someone called The Misfit.

Yet the stories absolutely are True, with a capital "T," if by True you mean they communicate eternal verities and bear the power to alter the real hearts of real people.

They altered my heart.

For me, then, Truth often is larger than anything a set of specific "facts" can show. I keep that in mind as I reread certain parts of the Bible, such as Genesis.

If there is a God, as I believe there is, he probably could have created the whole world in a six-day week. If he's God, he can do whatever he wants.

Did he do it that way? I don't know. I wasn't there. There seems to be a lot of evidence that it took much longer than six days. And even old St. Peter, in one of his New Testament epistles, points out that God doesn't measure time the way we do, that for God a day might actually be as a thousand years is to us.

When I read the opening chapters of Genesis, I don't care whether the account is factual. I don't care whether creation took a week or seven billion years.

I do hold that the story is True. Here's what it tells me:

- God set in motion the processes that formed us all.

- God intended the world to be a good place, stocked with abundant food for everyone, populated with people who cared deeply for him, the planet and one another.

- People—through their uncontrollable vanity and shortsightedness—made a mess of this wonderful potential.

- Today we still suffer for the sins of our forebears, while repeating their misdeeds over and over ourselves.

Granted, the first two Truths I accept by faith, by choice. But the latter two I can recognize from my own hard experiences in life.

CAREGIVING FROM THE PERSPECTIVE
OF A PATIENT

September 18, 2004

I've written a couple of columns lately about the toll that results from taking care of a seriously ill loved one over an extended period. As you probably know by now, my wife of twenty-five years, Renee, is battling advanced cancer.

But having written about the issues with which caregivers wrestle, I realized it would only be appropriate to tell the other side, too: the struggles of the sick themselves.

I decided to interview the person I consider the leading expert on that subject: Renee, who has survived more than four years longer than her doctors thought possible.

She has managed to (for the most part) keep her sanity in a situation that would have driven any lesser person over the edge. Her hospice nurse calls her a "one-in-a-million" patient, one who's disabled, desperately ill and yet not despondent.

Here's what it's like, according to my wife, to be this sick for this long, living every day under a potential death sentence:

• Renee was thirty-nine when doctors found that cancer had spread through her breasts, bones and lungs. She had always been unusually active, a supportive mother, a banker, our church's music director, a sports fan. Her condition deteriorated quickly; for several years now, she hasn't been able to do much of anything outside the home.

She "can't have a life," she says, which means she can't go to her old job, can't watch our son's rock band perform, can't attend church services, can't go out to eat comfortably, can't shop, can't take vacations.

In her head, she's still the same person she always was, with the same desires and interests. But she no longer recognizes the flesh she's confined to.

"That's real frustrating," she says. "My body doesn't want to cooperate with my mind. Therefore I find things to do with my mind."

She's read more books in the past four years than she did in the previous forty. She keeps the accounting records for our church's benevolence fund. She cross-stitches. She plays games on the computer. She watches TV. She takes correspondence courses.

• When she was healthy, Renee was herself a kind of caretaker, especially for our son and me. She cooked our favorite foods, made sure we had clean clothes, served as the girl Friday who kept up with all our social obligations.

Now she has to depend on us, and a few other family members, for everything. We prepare her meals and snacks, rent the DVDs she wants to watch, wash her pajamas, run her errands.

Being so totally dependent, even on family, is brutal, she says. She feels as if she's constantly imposing on us, and, at the same time, we (which is to say, mainly, I) don't handle matters the way she would have done them herself.

• By necessity, even most family members and close friends must get on with their business. A person as confined as Renee finds herself frequently alone or nearly so. That's unavoidable. Few people can sit by your sickbed for years on end.

But this still leaves her feeling out of the loop, isolated, forgotten. She wants to know what's happening at church or at her workplace or with her extended family. That doesn't change when you're ill, she says. Indeed a sick person might have even more of a need for basic chitchat because it distracts her from her own situation.

• Renee says it's too easy for her to lapse into anger, resentment, sadness and depression. To ward off these negative emotions, she relies on her faith, and particularly on the Bible: "I have to put my trust in the Lord and think about the Word."

She tries to discipline herself to obey this scriptural passage: "Whatever is true, whatever is noble, whatever is right, whatever is pure, whatever is lovely, whatever is admirable—if anything is excellent or praiseworthy—think about such things" (Philippians 4:8).

• Finally, she says, it's important to look for the humor—sometimes gallows humor—in life generally and in her own situation specifically. Laughter is therapeutic, she believes: "It really does help lift your spirits."

She makes fun of her own withered body. She makes even more fun of my feeble efforts to cook and clean.

There's nothing beneficial about a critical illness except this: Whether you're the caregiver or the ailing person, you learn a lot about yourself, others, God and life. Renee and I hope that what we're learning might help some of you through your own trials.

LOSING WIFE OFFERS LESSONS
IN CARRYING ON

May 28, 2005

On May 5, at 4:40 a.m.—exactly the time of morning our only child was born and two days after his twenty-second birthday—my wife, Renee, died.

Thus ended her five-year bout with cancer.

Renee passed away in a hospital bed in our den. Our son, John, sat in a chair beside her, holding her hand. I was rubbing her leg. Her mother and several other family members stood around us.

There were eerie coincidences. Renee had declined sharply in the last few days and nearly died on John's birthday; she almost lost her life on the anniversary of her having delivered life to our baby. In 1986, my maternal grandmother had died on his birthday.

Renee had initially fallen sick in 2000 while attending the Kentucky Derby; we buried her on Derby Day 2005. That was May 7, two years to the day from my mother's death. In 1968, my favorite grandfather, Papa Chestnut, died in May.

I've discovered I have little to say about losing Renee that doesn't sound like the usual clichés. But clichés become clichés because they contain certain elements of truth.

Here's one: I wasn't prepared for Renee to die. She'd long been under a death sentence. Yet, when she passed, I couldn't believe it was happening.

I kept waiting for her heart to start up again—for her to make a last-minute comeback. When she didn't, it took me as much by surprise as if she'd been perfectly healthy and killed in a car wreck. I'd thought I was braced for the end. I wasn't.

Here's another cliché: I'd considered that she probably wouldn't survive her illness, and I'd sometimes thought it would be a relief when the struggle finally ended. It isn't a relief at all. It's just a different kind of pain.

I delivered her eulogy myself because the minister she'd asked me to get was traveling out of state and couldn't reach Kentucky in time.

Besides, I figured I knew her better than anyone else. I told the crowd three things about her: she was one of the funniest people I knew; she was one of the most loving people I ever met; and she was, without question, the most faith-filled.

When she died, she had a jar of money on a table beside her bed in which she was collecting coins and small-denomination bills—for the trip to Hawaii she planned to take when she recovered. That's how much faith she had.

God missed a lot of good opportunities to heal her. I don't have any answers for that. All I know is that in life, as in high school football, sometimes you have to suck it up and go on. As her survivors, John and I are trying to do that. We're trudging forward into a strange world that no longer contains my wife and his mom.

The other night I was out late alone, taking a drive in the country because I was restless. Scanning the radio dial, I happened across one of those perpetually angry hosts of some conservative political show. She and her call-in guests were in the middle of the usual screed against the heathen, heartless, liberal media.

Here's the media I know: On Kentucky Derby weekend, the busiest weekend of the *Herald-Leader*'s year, a slew of my old friends there, including publisher Tim Kelly, drove to Mount Sterling to pay their respects to Renee, even though I haven't worked full-time at the newspaper in eight years and haven't set foot in the newsroom in two years. Staff writer Art Jester wrote a beautiful tribute to Renee on the obituaries page.

Other media folks visited the funeral home, too: Mike Embry, the editor of *Kentucky Monthly* magazine; Jack Pattie, the radio personality. Many journalists, some in Lexington and others scattered across the nation, called or sent cards or gifts.

That kind of outpouring counts when you're grieving. So let me recommend that you not approach me soon to rail against the media. A lot of those people have been nicer to me over the years than have many of the more pompous and self-righteous Christians I know. In fact, a fair number of those media folks are themselves Christians, although they tend not to be overbearing about it.

It's strange. Weeks have passed, but I don't feel unmarried yet. I wonder whether I ever will. I don't think I realized before this how much of my identity was wrapped up in Renee.

When I put on my clothes, I still catch myself thinking, "I need to ask Renee if this shirt and pants match." When I can't find my glasses, I think, "Renee will know where they are." When I get hungry, I think, "I wonder what Renee wants for supper."

Today, at least as I write these words, I'm not so much sad as I am just confused. I'm a middle-age guy, two-thirds of my life over, trying to figure out who I am.

Renee's not here to tell me.

GOD AND HIS HOUSE
DESERVE YOUR TITHES

June 25, 2005

I've heard a lot of people say that churches want members only for their money. In my observation, the folks who say this tend to be the same ones who wouldn't toss a nickel to charity if Mother Teresa herself rose from the grave and begged them.

Actually, most of the ministers I'm acquainted with hate to ask for money. They don't care a lot about money themselves (if they did they'd have chosen a more lucrative profession such as, say, teaching school or driving a Pepsi truck), and they really dread hearing their congregations grouse after yet another sermon on stewardship.

So allow me a word here on the poor preachers' behalf.

I not only believe you should give liberally to the church or temple you attend, I believe—and I hope you're sitting down—in the ancient law of tithing. Tithing means donating a full tenth of your income to your house of worship.

In fact, in a society as blessed as ours, a tenth ought to be the starting point for many of us. The higher your household income, the bigger a share of it you should give away. You owe God your eternal soul. Pay up.

There, I said it. OK, now, take a deep breath and wipe the oatmeal you just spit up off your shirt.

There are legitimate reasons why churches need your cash and equally legitimate reasons why you need to part with it generously.

First, religious organizations require buildings with roofs, running water, workbooks, buses, janitors, secretaries and clergy. The electric company doesn't accept a congregation's statement of faith as payment; it wants a check that doesn't bounce. If you prefer a clean sanctuary in which to worship or a minister who's available to come pray for you when you're about to be wheeled into heart surgery instead of spending his weekdays working as a greeter at Wal-Mart, then you ought to pay your dues.

Second, tithes support the less fortunate. My church, for instance, donates twelve percent of all the money it receives to missions and the needy. That twelve percent helps impoverished mothers in our community get their heat turned back on in the winter when they can't pay their bills. It goes for rice we ship to Christian organizations in Haiti, where extreme poverty and near-starvation are the norms of life.

Third, contributions make it possible to spread the good news. If you think Christianity (or in your case, perhaps, Judaism or Islam) has an important message to share, then keep in mind that it's difficult to get that message out unless you have trained clergy to present it, a pulpit from which they can speak and perhaps even airtime on TV or radio. You don't mind forking over a small fortune to HBO or the local cineplex so Hollywood can disseminate its views. Why would you recoil at helping your church spread a message of love, hope and eternal redemption?

Fourth, consistent tithing develops a healthy dose of self-discipline and self-denial. We live in a society that teaches us to focus constantly on what we want—a fifty-inch television with surround-sound speakers, so we can pretend we're in a movie theater even when we're sitting in our den eating potato chips.

That's why tithing isn't easy. You have to think about someone other than yourself. You might have to postpone buying that Harley you lust after in order to contribute to the greater good. You'll feel deprived in the short run but far better in the long run. If it doesn't hurt you to give, you're not giving enough. Remember the words of St. Paul, who was talking about giving money when he said: "For the one who sows to his own flesh shall from the flesh reap corruption."

Fifth, generous giving is a biblical commandment, discussed at length in both the Old and New Testaments. The Old Testament law demanded ten percent. In the New Testament, Jesus told his disciples to give away everything they owned. So think of it like this: if you go with the Old Testament tithe, you're actually getting off easy.

Finally, we're told that God himself loves cheerful givers as opposed to misers—and rewards them accordingly. Back to St. Paul: "He who sows sparingly shall also reap sparingly; and he who sows bountifully shall also reap bountifully." There have been times when I thought I couldn't afford to give my tithe.

Then I'd realize that the truth is, I can't afford not to.

TRYING TO FIGURE OUT
THE REST OF MY LIFE

July 09, 2005

Near the end of his autobiography, *My Life*, Bill Clinton tells of a rock he kept in a glass case in the Oval Office. Astronauts had brought it back from the moon in 1969, and carbon-dating tests had determined it to be 3.6 billion years old.

When tensions among his advisers rose, Clinton recalls, he would interrupt their arguments by pointing to the moon rock. He'd remind everyone of its extraordinary age.

"We're all just passing through," he'd say. "Let's calm down and go back to work."

That's a terrific lesson in perspective. Perspective is something I'm trying mightily to hold onto these days.

I have no desire to become a professional widower, to write about my loss over and again. I'm not particularly self-indulgent, and I'm not a masochist. But frankly, losing Renee is the matter still foremost in my thoughts.

My grief is unusual, though, only in that I have this column in which to publicly express it. Every day, when I pick up the newspaper, I see dozens of obituaries. Every name was somebody's wife or husband or son or father or sister. Every day, people lose family. It's the way of mankind. Realizing that offers a kind of perspective as well.

There's a great multitude of bereaved folks out there. Most of them get through it eventually. They cope. They go back to their work. So will I, I suppose. So will my son. So will my wife's parents. I know that.

In the meantime, each new day brings its own unique set of questions and regrets.

Here's what my situation feels like today. I'm almost fifty—a half-century old, which is hard for me to comprehend. And for the first time since I was twenty-one, I'm free to do exactly as I please. Yet when friends ask what I intend to do, I confess, "I don't know."

I'm still young enough to have options. I'm in comparatively decent health for a middle-age guy with an incurable fondness for Krispy Kremes. I'm financially solvent. I could reinvent myself. But I'm not sure what I'd become.

Friends ask, do I want to continue preaching?

Probably. That's been my vocation for decades. I think I'm called to it. But at present, I feel mentally and spiritually more like I'm seventy-nine than forty-nine. I've already said from the pulpit everything I know—and besides, I don't know nearly as much as I used to. Perhaps my congregation needs new blood.

Would I rather devote myself to full-time writing?

Possibly. I have ideas for several books about various historical events. Researching them would require me to travel and to think about matters other than my own problems. Yet, writing books provides at best an erratic, and for most authors a miniscule, income. And sooner or later, I'd need a steady job.

Will I ever remarry?

Maybe. I already miss—so much it's impossible to explain—that intimacy a husband and wife can share. I see something funny in town and there's no one to tell when I go home. I worry at night and there's no one to confide in. I'd hate to think there'll never be anyone there again.

But the only thing that depresses me worse than being alone is my vision of being out in the dating world. My observation is that usually the women you want most don't want you. The ones who want you, you don't want.

If and when you do marry somebody you love and who loves you equally, you've still got to solve the myriad issues that stem from the two of you having different idiosyncrasies and sleep patterns and goals. It took Renee and me ten years to work through all that junk. Loving a woman and living with her are entirely different matters.

Maybe I'll just get a dog instead. If you put food in its dish, a dog tends to think you're wonderful. I have food.

Gee, it's a big, crazy world. But it always has been. Throughout the ages, people have argued and loved and lusted and suffered, and at last, died. And their survivors wept and then pressed on until they, too, returned to dust.

Clinton ends his anecdote about the moon rock by saying: "Our job is to live as well and as long as we can, and to help others to do the same. What happens after that, and how we're viewed by others, is beyond our control. The river of time carries us all away. All we have is the moment."

That's absolutely true.

Even so, my earlier moments were far easier to live in than this one.

LOVE THY NOXIOUS NEIGHBOR?

July 23, 2005

When I finally lose what's left of my sanity, it won't be because of some cataclysmic event—not a terrorist attack or a cholera outbreak or the collapse of the economy. When I go crazy, it'll be because That One Person sent me over the edge.

You know the One I'm talking about—that one goofball at every public event who ruins the experience for everyone else.

What's this got to do with faith and values?

That One Person has, over and again, nearly made me lose my religion. And apparently, That One Person missed the lessons in basic civility the rest of us absorbed in Sunday school or in second grade.

I've been taking notes on That One Person—I really have—trying to discover any patterns of age, gender, place of birth or race that set That One apart. There isn't a pattern. I've encountered That One Person from my small Kentucky town to as far away as New Orleans, where my son and I recently vacationed:

• Mount Sterling theater. My son, his girlfriend and I are watching *War of the Worlds*.

That One Person: Woman, about thirty-five, sitting behind us.

Her cell phone rings three times during the film. Each time, she answers the call and proceeds to engage in lengthy conversations.

What I'm thinking: "Lady, do you have a speaking part in this film? If not, then shut up!"

• Mule-drawn carriage ride, New Orleans.

That One Person: Woman, about fifty, from New Jersey (she declares her home state at the ride's onset).

69

Our driver, an entertaining fellow named Primetime, supplies us with friendly patter about the French Quarter, patter we can barely hear because That One Person is talking incessantly to her husband about everything from the weather to who she plans to invite to their Thanksgiving dinner this fall.

Primetime says, "To your right is Cafe du Monde, where you can get world famous beignets and chicory coffee."

That One Person, loudly: "Where is it? What's it called?"

Primetime says, "Now, up ahead, is the notorious House of the Rising Sun."

That One Person: "When are we going to see the House of the Rising Sun?"

Primetime: "Right here, ma'am."

That One Person: "Honey, it's the House of the Rising Sun! Stop the carriage, driver! I want to take pictures!"

Primetime says, "This building once housed a U.S. mint."

That One Person, to her husband, even more loudly: "Didn't he say earlier the mule's name is Barney? My grandfather had a mule named Barney!" (The mule's name is Bessie.)

What I'm thinking: "Your poor husband."

•   Oak Alley Plantation, southern Louisiana.

That One Person: Guy with northern accent, about forty. We're about to tour the plantation house.

Our hostess, a young Southern woman who looks as if she's working her way through college, says, "Welcome to Oak Alley. Y'all come right on in, and we'll get started."

That One Person declares, in a snide tone: "Y'all come on in, y'all. Hee hee!"

What I'm thinking: "Slick, one more peep from you, and y'all are liable to get y'all's hind end kicked by a couple of good ol' Kentucky boys."

•   Same tour, Oak Alley Plantation.

That One Person: Guy, about twenty-five.

With several companions, he barges into the mansion's closed parlor, five minutes into our hostess's talk. Tells everyone, happily, "Here we are! Late arrivals!" He then delivers his own monologue over the top of our hostess's, from room to room throughout the remainder of the tour, laughing shrilly at his own witticisms.

What I'm thinking: "Why don't you stand over beside that other obnoxious guy? That way we can kick both of y'all's hind ends at the same time."

- Swamp tour by boat, rural Louisiana.

That One Person: Woman, about sixty-five.

Our guide is telling us thrilling tales about alligators, snakes and Cajuns. That One Person's cell phone rings throughout the two-hour ride. She doesn't turn it off—and doesn't ever answer it.

What I'm thinking: "If that phone rings again, I'm snatching it out of your purse and tossing it to the gators."

- Interstate 40, Tennessee, coming home.

That One Person: Driver of minivan, invisible behind tinted glass.

Pulls into the passing lane and stays there for ten miles, driving sixty miles an hour in a seventy mph zone. Has traffic backed up as far as the eye can see. Van's bumper sticker: "Jesus is the answer."

What I'm thinking: "If Jesus answers me, he'll push you into the slow lane where you belong, you inconsiderate yo-yo."

In closing, you should always remember, gentle readers, that God is love.

It's why I haven't strangled That One Person. Yet.

NEW ORLEANS TRIP ILLUSTRATES
UNCERTAINTY OF LIFE

September 10, 2005

Two months ago, my son and I took a vacation to New Orleans. Having spent five years providing care for my terminally ill wife, John and I agreed we deserved to splurge. I booked us a room in a luxury hotel downtown, on the edge of the French Quarter and a few blocks from the Superdome. We had a magnificent view of the Mississippi.

As we arrived, Hurricane Dennis was blowing strong out in the Gulf of Mexico and was believed to be headed full-force for the city. During our stay, the hotel's concierge monitored the storm's approach on a computer. John and I struck up a brief friendship with her. We'd stop by her desk to catch the latest news.

She explained the hotel's procedures for keeping its guests safe and comfortable during a hurricane. She let us come around behind her desk so we could see the Doppler graphics and weather reports she was getting. She told us her dad worked for the National Weather Service and that she was checking with him by phone to supplement the information available on-line.

Meanwhile, the skies over the French Quarter remained sunny. As we wandered the streets, taking in their exotic sights, John and I decided it would be huge fun to stay in the Big Easy when the hurricane struck. We would hole up in our fancy hotel while the winds howled and the rains whipped the sidewalks outside. What a great story we'd come home with. It would be scary, but only to about the same extent that a roller-coaster ride is scary—you know that, in the end, you're going to walk away in one piece; plans have been made for your survival.

I assumed that no storm could do truly catastrophic damage to a major American city in the 21st century. By coincidence, I happened to be reading myself to sleep at night with *Isaac's Storm*, a book about the 1900 hurricane that demolished Galveston, Texas, and killed thousands of people—and every night I'd comfort myself with the knowledge that modern buildings, sea walls and urban infrastructures are infinitely better prepared to withstand the forces of nature than they were a century ago.

John and I left New Orleans without seeing so much as a lightning flash. Dennis veered off toward Florida and wore itself out.

Now I realize how stupid we were. The neighborhood we stayed in, the streets we walked, lately are nightmarish CNN visions of Katrina's apocalypse: flooding, drowning, hunger, thirst, shooting, looting, desperation of all kinds. Like everyone, I'm sickened by the carnage. I'm appalled at the government's lack of preparation and its inept responses.

I've also been thinking about how close John and I came to being victims in that hell. If Dennis had zigged instead of zagged, or if we had visited New Orleans in late August rather than in early July, we might have found ourselves among all those wretched sufferers I now watch on TV from the comfort of my air-conditioned home in Kentucky. A few days here or there, a few arbitrary twists of wind, and we might be dead or maimed. Our lives could have been hurled onto a completely different course.

The other night John, who is only twenty-two and thus still of the conviction that he is the epicenter of the universe, put forth the idea that maybe God moved Dennis away from New Orleans just to spare the two of us.

I told him I'm not quite that egotistical anymore. I don't imagine that he and I are more special to God than many others among those thousands who were killed or displaced by Katrina. I imagine that some of those folks actually were better people than we are, and probably on terms with the Almighty superior to ours. If God didn't turn aside Katrina for them, he probably didn't turn aside Dennis for us.

I am indeed thankful that, for whatever reasons, we escaped. We've only begun to emerge from a five-year disaster of our own. We certainly didn't need another.

Still, the only lesson I can draw from our near-miss in New Orleans is an old one: Life is uncertain. Very uncertain.

A tiny, innocuous-looking bump on your chest can turn out to be a harmless cyst—or it can turn out to be cancer. Vacations to major U.S. cities can be amusing diversions—until one becomes a historic tragedy.

I remember for the 10,000th time that I should spend each day doing the things I love, as if it were my last day on Earth. Because it might well be.

And I should live prepared to vault into eternity sooner than I'd planned. Because I might find myself in eternity at any moment, without prior notice.

THE SAME BAD DAY, OVER AND OVER

September 24, 2005

I get the feeling there's a lesson I'm supposed to learn. But I must be a slow learner, because I keep having to cover the same material over and over again.

Five-and-a-half years now, I've been acting in my own private version of *Groundhog Day*, the movie in which Bill Murray endlessly relives one awful day.

Last week, my dad was walking into a Taco Bell for lunch. He tripped over the curb, fell into the glass door and broke his upper arm in three places. An ambulance rushed him to the hospital.

Now he's at home, nearly immobilized. He can't change his clothes or take a bath or wash his hair or get his food. He can't sleep in a bed—he has to sit up all night in a recliner. He can't be left alone, because his strength is questionable and his balance is worse. If the broken arm weren't enough, he's almost seventy-five and a severe diabetic.

So my sister, my brother-in-law and I are sharing caregiving duties. One of us has to be with Dad around the clock, while juggling all our other obligations. We'll be doing this for a few weeks at least, and maybe more, depending on his rate of recovery.

Just two years ago, the same three of us were taking turns sitting up all night with my poor mother as she was dying of cancer.

And as my mom passed away, my wife, Renee, was waging her own battle with cancer, which she lost in May. Most of those years, she was desperately sick. We had help from hospice and family and church members. But mainly the burden of seeing to her needs fell to me.

For years, then, my life has consisted of nursing incapacitated family members. I've learned to cook. I've learned to iron. I've washed other people's hair. I've given baths. I've emptied catheter bags and bedside potties. I've wiped butts. I've mopped up vomit and blood. I've slept on lumpy cots and uncomfortable chairs.

For years on end. For years seemingly without end. I thought it was finally over when Renee died, but now it's started up again.

My sister once made me a T-shirt. It says: "This is not the life I ordered."

Amen, sister.

My own line is that I've learned a lot of truths about myself—none of which I ever wanted to know. It turns out there's a great chasm between the person I wish I were and the person I am.

Because the truth is, I hate all this.

Until Renee got sick in 2000, I used to believe I was the luckiest guy I ever knew. I had a beautiful wife who adored me, an ample income, jobs I enjoyed, good health. I couldn't figure out what I'd done to deserve such a bounty.

Since 2000 I've had a lot of luck, too. All of it terrible. I can't figure out what I've done to deserve that, either. I wonder if God's developed a grudge against me.

The other night, two of Renee's sisters invited me over for supper. I walked in and without thinking plopped down at the table. One of my sisters-in-law went to the kitchen, fixed me a drink and a plate of food and set them before me. I almost started crying. I couldn't remember the last time anyone had waited on me. It felt so good I couldn't bear it. And it felt sad to find myself so moved by such a simple act.

I should be grateful that I'm still blessed with a modicum of health myself, that when my dad is feeble, I'm able to lift him from his chair. But I discover that what I really want is to run screaming from the house.

I should feel sorry for Renee and my mom and my dad—for all they've suffered and endured. And I do feel bad for them, really I do, every day. I didn't want them to suffer at all. But honestly I find myself feeling equally sorry, if not more sorry, for Paul.

I should treasure the opportunity to serve those I love; I should feel privileged to sit close beside them during their declining days. But often I worry instead about whether anybody will be left to sit beside me when my own hour comes. Maybe after seeing all of them to their rewards, I'll die alone in some foul-smelling nursing home.

The hardest thing I've had to learn about myself, then, is just how self-centered I can be. Ultimately, it's all about me. I expected better of myself.

If there's any other lesson I'm supposed to be getting here, some great truth beyond the obvious fact that I'm egocentric, I've apparently missed it.

None of it makes much sense. Sometimes in life, you get to do what you want, and other times you wake up in the mornings, steel yourself and do what you have to.

CHOOSING TO BE SELFLESS,
NOT SELFISH

November 12, 2005

At a bookstore one night, I ran into a former professor of mine. He knew I'd lost my wife. "So, what are you going to do with the rest of your life?" he said.

"I don't know," I said. "I really don't know."

A few days later, I went to church for our regular Wednesday spaghetti supper. Shortly after I sat down at a table among several friends, someone else ushered in a homeless man toting a backpack and invited him to eat with us.

As the guy eagerly filled up his plate, a buddy sitting next to me said, "Oh, I'm so glad he came in."

She said she'd passed the man on the highway. She'd wanted to stop and ask if he needed a meal but decided it wasn't wise for a woman alone to pick up a drifter.

Then she turned to me. "I started to call you and tell you to pick him up on your way out here, but then I thought, 'No, Paul's not going to pick up some homeless guy. He'll tell me to take a pill and calm down.'"

She said this humorously. But many a truth has been said in jest. The fact was, I'd also seen the guy walking down the highway. I'd thought about stopping—for a half second. Then I drove by. I figured his problems were none of my business.

What she said bothered me. My lack of compassion apparently is so visible that my friends know what I'm not going to do before I know it myself: Paul won't stop for the homeless guy.

When I was younger, I used to believe that if I could ever become a published writer, I'd die happy. That would be the height of self-fulfillment for me. Over the years I've done a lot of writing. I've been published in newspapers and magazines and anthologies. I've written books. I've won awards. I get fan mail. It's all very nice.

I've learned that each new accomplishment leaves me really satisfied with myself—for about an hour. Then it's back to being plain old me again. None of that lasts. It's like drinking too much. You feel ten feet tall. Then you sober up.

On the other hand, I've managed, occasionally, to do a few things that have brought me lasting rewards.

I knew a young guy who got in trouble with the law and was sentenced to prison. He turned to me for help, and I decided to oblige. I visited him in jail several times, counseled him, prayed with him. I told the prosecutor I thought the kid could be redeemed. The prosecutor talked with the judge, and they decided to take a chance. They released him on shock probation after he'd served only a few months.

One condition for his release was that he promised to continue hanging out with me. We became pals. Over time, I watched him change. He married a wonderful young woman. He started his own small business, which has been successful. He and his wife have a couple of kids. He's now an elder in my church. He's scrupulously honest.

Every time I see him, I smile inside. I'm not responsible for his turnaround. He had God's help, and other people's help, and he made a lot of excellent decisions himself.

But I did my little part. I tried. And my trying made a difference. He's told me that repeatedly.

The problem is, such deeds are decidedly the exceptions in my life, as my church friend amiably, and accurately, brought to my attention.

I've thought a lot lately about that, and about my old professor's question: What do I want to do with the rest of my life?

I've realized—or maybe I've simply remembered what I once knew and forgot—that the only things you do that have lasting value and leave you feeling good for more than a few minutes are the things you do for other people.

You shouldn't do kind deeds just to make yourself feel noble. You ought to do them for the sake of the people you're helping. But doing good makes you feel good anyway. That's a byproduct of the overall process. And it makes others feel good about you. Simply put, good deeds live on. They have an afterlife for all concerned.

So here's what I want to do with my life: I want to live less selfishly.

We're all on our way off this planet. I might have a year or forty years, but someday sooner than I'd prefer, I'll be gone. While I'm here I want to be a giver.

I hope that when finally I'm on display in my coffin, folks will look down on my powdered corpse and say, "Well, there lies old Paul, bless his heart. He was a genuine Christian. When people were in trouble, he always helped."

WHAT WE LEAVE BEHIND

February 11, 2006

In one of several cardboard boxes in my living room, beside the bookcase and near the hearth, sit an old ceramic mother cat and her kitten.

Somewhere along the line, somebody accidentally knocked a slot about an inch long through the mama cat's back, so that now she looks like a child's coin bank, which she isn't. There used to be two kittens; one of them has disappeared.

My dad's dad, Fred Prather, gave the cats to my granny, Lennie, as a wedding present. They were married Dec. 23, 1916, in Pulaski County. Fred and Lennie have long since gone to their glory, but these two cats remain, marred and chipped a bit, yet otherwise intact.

I imagine my grandfather bought them for a few cents at a general store or a dime store. He passed through this world without earning, much less saving, any money to speak of, and I doubt he could have paid much for them.

Yet those cheap ceramic cats are here. My grandparents are in their graves. A knickknack has lasted ninety years. Few people do.

I've spent the past months sorting through the flotsam of my loved ones' lives. It's interesting, and perplexing, and sad, to handle the detritus we humans accumulate and then leave behind.

Each item in my cardboard boxes clearly was important in its time, cherished enough to be held onto in life and passed down in death, in some cases generation after generation. I think we've kept such relics for overlapping reasons: out of duty, out of memorial, out of love, out of laziness.

Not long ago, a friend helped me unpack those boxes, examine their contents, repack them. The experience got us both thinking. Every estate sale is somebody's tragedy, she observed. Every week in our town, trunks, dishes and carefully folded linens are set out to be picked

81

over by strangers. Their true owners—their true meanings, their histories—have vanished on eternity's winds.

My house is cluttered with mementos, in boxes, in stacked photo albums, on various shelves, in closets and corners.

There's an oak high chair. My maternal grandfather, Oscar Chestnut, sat in it as a baby. My mother ate from that same chair. Later still, so did I. The fuzzy brown hat and hand muff my mom wore as a preschooler rest atop the high chair's tray.

A battered hand bell stands on the mantle over the fireplace. It once called children in from recess at the two-room Oak Hill School near Somerset, where both Papa Chestnut and my mom attended elementary school. Somehow the bell ended up in my family. The teachers who swung it and the children it called are now dead.

I have our family's Bible, its register inscribed with dates going back more than a century: relatives born, married, buried. I knew some of these names as breathing, talking, laughing men and women; heard of others through stories told by my parents and grandparents. I have no idea who other names were, but they were no less human, no less excited and fretting and hopeful.

I have my great-grandparents' wedding photograph. I have photographs of my own wedding in 1978. I have photographs of my wife, Renee, as a young, grinning mother, of my son as a baby. I have the figurines of angels Renee kept displayed near her sickbed, from which she drew inspiration during her illness. I have her spiral-bound prayer journals. I have birthday and Valentine's cards we gave each other.

In my kitchen cabinet is a small blue bowl, stacked among all the other bowls. My Grandma Chestnut baked the most delicious chocolate pies I've ever eaten. She'd dip the leftover filling into that blue bowl and let me slurp it up as warm pudding.

A day will come when all those keepsakes will be thrown in the garbage or sold at auction. Each item meant something special to a person I loved. Each item remains precious to me. And all those keepsakes, taken together, mean nothing.

Centuries ago, a preacher told the true story: "Vanity of vanities," he said. "All is vanity and striving after wind."

BLESSED AND TROUBLED
ARE THE CAREGIVERS

March 25, 2006

When singer-actress Dana Reeve died this month at forty-four, I wondered how much her late husband's nine-year disability contributed to her own early demise.

Reeve succumbed to lung cancer. News reports said she was a non-smoker. She had, however, nursed her husband, the actor Christopher Reeve, from the horse-riding accident in 1995 that left him a quadriplegic until his death in October 2004.

Perhaps these two things—Dana Reeve's years of caregiving and her fatal illness—were unrelated. No one can say for sure. Cancer remains a mysterious disease, and no one has ever determined that it can be caused by fatigue or emotional turmoil.

However, having been a round-the-clock nurse to my wife, my first thought on reading of Reeve's passing was, "The caregiving got her."

That's not such a wild leap. In February, an Associated Press reporter wrote an unsettling article about a study of 518,240 caregivers, conducted at Harvard University and the University of Pennsylvania and backed by the National Institutes of Health. The study initially was published in the prestigious *New England Journal of Medicine*.

Researchers found that a spouse's debilitating illness often hastens the death of the caregiving husband or wife. They blamed, in the summary of Associated Press reporter Jeff Donn, "stress and the loss of companionship, practical help, income and other support that can occur when a spouse gets sick."

The chief researcher, Dr. Nicholas Christakis of Harvard, told Donn, "You can die of a broken heart not just when a partner dies, but when your partner falls ill."

This particular study looked at elderly caregivers. But my experiences tell me the issues they face aren't that different from those confronting Dana Reeve. Or you. Or me.

Researchers found that older men are 4.5 percent more likely than usual to die on any given day after their wives are hospitalized, and women with sick husbands are about three percent more likely to die.

The risks run especially high if the spouse's disease is severely disabling—a stroke, heart attack, pneumonia or hip fracture—or if the sick person suffers from dementia or mental problems.

In those intensive situations, the caregiver's risk of death multiplies—up to fifty-eight percent higher than normal for men and seventy-seven percent for women.

And if a sick spouse actually dies, the survivor often quickly succumbs to an accident, suicide, infection or complications from conditions such as diabetes.

Quoting Christakis again from the Associated Press: "What it means to me is that people are interconnected, and so their health is interconnected, and in really real ways, there can be a kind of spread of diseases between people."

To me, this is irrefutably true. During the five years of my wife's illness, which required constant caregiving, I developed both diabetes and high blood pressure.

When I was a full-time newspaper reporter, co-workers used to rib me about being incurably upbeat in the newsroom, an environment not known for its optimists. Yet during Renee's sickness, I fell into clinical depression. For roughly two years, I took a prescription antidepressant. It saved what's left of my sanity.

A Christian counselor told me I actually fared better than many long-term caregivers, even those who are deeply religious. Disproportionately, he said, caregivers tend to abuse drugs or alcohol, to have extramarital affairs or to simply climb in their cars and drive away, never to be heard from again.

(Lest you worry, I'm OK now. My diabetes and hypertension are under control. I'm no longer depressed and have no need for an antidepressant.)

I always think twice before I write about the stresses of caregiving. Some of you who read this column are the sick husbands or wives being cared for; I hate to add to your pain by pointing out the toll your illness might exact on your spouse.

I'm aware of how soul-crushing it can be to lie in bed, dependent on others. It's been ten months since Renee died, and I still cry thinking about all she suffered.

But it's needful, I believe, to point out that an extended, debilitating illness is about as difficult for the caregiver as it is for the disabled person.

I want churches, friends, extended families and medical workers to understand that caregivers need compassion and attention as much as the visibly ill do.

And I want you caregivers to know that the terrible, conflicted emotions you feel—empathy, loneliness, guilt, grief, fear, rage, inadequacy—aren't sinful, but are common to those who find themselves nursing people they deeply love. God bless you.

AFTER A YEAR, I'M STILL SORTING IT OUT

May 13, 2006

I still live in the same house. I drive the same car. With a few exceptions, I wear the same clothes. I have the same friends. I attend the same church. I read the same Bible.

Nearly everything is the same as before.

Except everything is different.

A year ago, on May 5, 2005, my wife, Renee, died. A year is supposed to mark a turning point in the grieving process, or so the experts say.

I haven't decided whether that's true. There are some ways in which I feel much better than I did in the weeks just after Renee passed away. There are other ways in which losing her hurts worse now than it did then.

On this first anniversary of her death, I live on two parallel planes.

There's the exterior me, which apparently appears to others, and occasionally to myself, as if I'm recovering. My friends rarely talk to me about Renee anymore or ask how I am. They must assume I'm OK.

Every morning, I brush my teeth, take my pills. I pull on a pair of jeans and drive downtown to my buddy Gary's shop for coffee. I field complaints from tenants who rent my apartments, prepare sermons, write newspaper columns, order films from NetFlix, exchange e-mails. I talk about the weather with clerks at Wal-Mart.

Then there's the interior me. This part reminds me of what John Prine says in one of his songs: "I could build me a castle with memories, just to have somewhere to go."

My recliner sits in the corner of our den where Renee's hospital bed used to be. It's the corner in which she died before my eyes. When I'm watching television there, I imagine what she'd say about the

86

particular show that's on, if she were still alive. She never lacked opinions—many of which I shared, and a few of which I didn't.

Last Sunday, I was watching my favorite series, *The Sopranos*. I remembered Renee fuming, "They cuss too much. That language is totally unnecessary." I smiled. She said that about every *Sopranos* episode. Back then, it annoyed me. Today, I'd give away everything I own to hear her say it one more time.

I've stood in church, looked toward the stage at the worship team—and seen Renee leading the singing again.

These memories, they've become my constant companions.

Don't misunderstand me. My life isn't all despair and gloom. I laugh frequently. And loudly. I have my son, John. My money's holding out. My health's adequate. I do pretty much as I want.

So yes, despite losing Renee, in many ways I'm blessed. I've heard about people who've lost three or four family members to a mass murderer. I know folks who are alone, impoverished and desperately sick.

Still. Here's what it's like at my house, a year later.

The other evening, long after midnight, I lay in bed with the light on, reading. My son knocked on my door. He's six-foot-three, a college senior.

I told him to come in. He opened the door, stood there a second, hesitant.

"Are you missing Mom?" he said.

I closed my book. "Yeah."

"Me, too."

Then he crawled in bed beside me, like he used to when he was a little boy. We talked into the wee hours, simply to hear each other's voices, trying to cover the big gaping holes in both our hearts.

There's never an hour—there's hardly a second—that Renee isn't on my mind. Wherever I am, whatever I'm doing, she's there. She's in my DNA.

And yet she's gone, forever. I understand that. I'm dealing with it as best I know how. Every day, I put one foot in front of the other.

Life goes on.

Until one day it doesn't.

YES, I QUESTION; SO DID DAVID, JOB

May 27, 2006

I want to say a bit more about having lost Renee before I move on from this subject for a season.

People ask me whether that ordeal—her decline and death, my caregiving and grief—has caused me to question God and my Christian faith. Some ask sympathetically. Some ask accusingly, as if I'll admit to having disgraced my pulpit, to having become an apostate. A few ask almost hopefully, as if they want me to join them in unbelief.

Yes, what our family endured has led me to question God and my church's teachings. Lord knows I'm not about to apologize for that, to him or anyone else.

I've never met anybody with as much calm faith as Renee had. I've got the personal journals she left behind. In the midst of suffering and loneliness, she wrote constantly about her love for the Lord and her total trust that he would heal her body.

She laboriously transcribed audiotapes from supposed prophets who'd promised her that God would grant her a miracle. They all had "words from the Lord" for her.

She withered away until she was helpless and emaciated, then died.

Some folks have told me, "God did heal her. Now she's every whit whole—she's in heaven." They mean well, but they don't understand. Renee longed to be physically healed here and now. She wanted to live. She had plenty to do on Earth. She ached to see her grandchildren someday. I exhausted myself praying for her recovery. Others prayed.

God didn't answer.

Face that, I say. Deal with it. If witnessing that doesn't rattle your beliefs, then you're either stupid, scared or a fraud. If your faith is so fragile you can't question it even when it appears not to work, even when God allows the person you love most to die painfully and needlessly—then you didn't have much faith anyway.

To me, genuine faith should be able to ask hard questions and to demand real answers, whether or not the answers ever arrive.

If what you've believed is indeed the truth, the truth always can stand up to scrutiny. And if what you've believed won't survive examination, why would you want to hold onto it? Who wants to entrust his eternal destiny to a myth?

In my view, God's big enough to handle my questions without falling apart or seeking vengeance on me. I'm able to cope when my son is perplexed with me. Should I imagine that Almighty God is pettier than I am?

The Bible itself is full of prophets, kings and preachers—and I'm talking about its heroes, not its goats—who railed at God, who impugned his credibility, and yet were declared righteous. That list is illustrious: Elijah, David, Job, Jeremiah, Jonah. They all asked, "God, where were you when I needed you?"

Even Jesus cried out, "My God, my God, why have you forsaken me?"

Questioning God or the tenets of your faith isn't synonymous with losing your faith. Questioning your faith doesn't define you as an infidel—at least, apparently, in God's judgment. And his judgment is the only one that matters.

Another, related question people ask is whether I'm angry with God.

No. I'm disappointed with him, but not angry. I hoped God would grant us a miracle, but I never felt he was obligated to do so. He's God, and I'm not.

However, I have been angry with a slew of God's servants. Over the past half-dozen years, I've seen the absolute best from Christians—and the absolute nadir. I've lost faith in many people. I've been equally, perhaps more, disgusted with myself.

Now I'm being forced to learn the virtue of forgiveness. Judge not, I remind myself. Forgive their trespasses and God will forgive yours.

Forgiveness is a choice. I've decided to forgive them all. That's the Gospel as best I'm able to comprehend it.

I forgive the people who've said the real reason Renee died was because she had hidden sin in her life, or because I, as her husband, didn't pray enough (as if my praying day and night for years on end wasn't sufficient to get God's attention, as if God has attention deficit disorder). I've been dumbfounded and wounded by the sheer pride, hypocrisy and meanness of things Christians have said.

Still, the Gospel demands I forgive them all and love them anyway.

I'm working on it. For I, too, stand in need of forgiveness and love. While I'm forgiving others, I also choose to forgive myself, for my own self-centeredness, frailty and surliness. That might be my toughest task.

Today, most of my questions about Renee's death remain unanswered. Maybe they always will. I don't understand God as thoroughly as I once thought I did.

I do, however, believe in God. And I believe, more strongly than ever, in the redeeming power of forgiveness and love.

RELIGIOUS PETTINESS
TRIES MY PATIENCE

June 10, 2006

I'm the pastor of a church—but I can't stand religion.

When I say I can't stand religion, I don't mean I can't stand people who are devout Christians or, for that matter, devout Jews or Hindus.

What I mean is, I dislike all sects and individuals who are consumed with self-righteousness, petty religious regulations and condescension toward those who don't precisely share their beliefs. I consider all those traits man-made, not God-made. Such attitudes keep more people away from God than they ever draw to him.

Jesus himself loathed religious people. In the Gospels, he never seems to get angry with prostitutes or crooked tax collectors. But he explodes regularly at the Pharisees, a bunch of hyper-religious wonks who think they're perfect.

It irritates me when people decide that because they belong to some particular denomination or pray eighty times a day or have been born again or speak in tongues, they're holier than anyone else.

I don't like people who think they've got all the answers. I don't like people who define their faith solely in terms of what they're against: dancing, TV, beer, rap music, movies, liberals, homosexuals or conservatives. Turn off the bile tap. Get a life.

(Of course, you might point out that I'm at this very moment defining my own faith in terms of what I'm against—religious prigs. You got me there. I plead guilty.)

Because I don't hew to typical religious stereotypes, people who meet me for the first time generally don't believe I'm an ordained minister at all.

For one thing, I don't look ministerial. I rarely wear a necktie to church. It's not a spiritual statement; ties choke me. My weekday uniform tends toward cargo shorts and golf shirts.

"Are you really a preacher?" people ask me.

Yes. But I don't think God cares much about our outward appearance. When God created people, he created them in a state of nature. That lets us know how important clothes are to him. I don't intend to walk around as naked as Adam—and I assure you, no one wants to see me do that—but I don't feel compelled to get all gussied up, either.

I'm not against those who do dress up. There's room in God's kingdom for all kinds. God apparently enjoys variety. He made apples. But he knew some folks wouldn't like apples, so he gave us bananas, too. And peaches and pears.

Faith is the same way. He knew some people would love Catholicism. But others wouldn't, so he created Methodists. He created people who enjoy dressing to the nines and others who prefer dressing like bums.

Then he created me, a kumquat in the kingdom of God—not terribly popular, occasionally acidic, an acquired taste. Still, he made me as I am.

So I'm not against pomp in church or colorful robes or beautiful sanctuaries. I don't care whether you sing Gregorian chants, recite the Apostles' Creed or fall on the floor in a Holy Ghost swoon—there's a place for each of us. Whatever works for you.

Just don't imagine you're holier than anyone else because you wear fancier clothes or speak in a more formal diction or pray more loudly.

To me, pure and undefiled religion—the real thing—is about establishing a relationship, a friendship, with God. It's about exhibiting love, forgiveness and mercy toward other human beings. It's not about clothes, picky rules or politics.

It's about recognizing your own sinfulness and inconsistencies. It's about being honest with God, yourself and others about who you really are.

I am who I am. Recently, I spoke at a communitywide service. In my talk, I mentioned a funny trait of my late wife's. She could never get any common saying right.

Once when she was driving, we got stuck behind another car whose driver sat immovable after the traffic light had turned green. Renee honked the horn and yelled: "Lady, either pee the pot or use it!"

After my talk, an audience member came up. He said, "That was an, uhm, interesting story about your wife—I can't believe you used the word 'pee' in a public address. Would you tell that story to your church from your own pulpit?"

"Would I?" I said. "I *have* told it from my pulpit."

If I read his expression correctly, he looked at me as if I were from Mars—or from some secret pocket of Hades where they train bad, irreverent preachers.

Yes, I'm a minister. But I talk like a real person, dress like a real person, think like a real person—because I am a real person. I can't figure out at what point being a Christian came to be equated with being uptight, prim and proper. Weren't all the original disciples rough fishermen or knotheads of other, similar sorts?

I love God. But religion wears on my brain and vexes my soul.

MY SON WAS MY ROCK
DURING HIS MOM'S ILLNESS

June 24, 2006

The longer I live, the less I believe in heroes. But I do know a very few people I consider genuinely heroic.

At the top of that list is my son, John.

Recently I wrote here that I intended to leave for a while the topic of my late wife's fatal illness, but earlier I'd asked to interview John, age twenty-three, for a column about his views of the trials our family endured. At the time I asked, he declined.

Then he changed his mind. He said he had a few observations worth passing on. That's why I'm back to a column on caregiving and grief.

John, our only child, turned seventeen a week before Renee was diagnosed with inoperable cancer in May 2000. He was finishing his junior year in high school. Renee and I asked little from him during her sickness. We realized he was a kid.

Yet for five years, he fed his mom, massaged her, sat up nights keeping her company. He passed up the chance to go away to college—choosing to commute, so he could be with us. He loved us both unconditionally.

Whenever I got exhausted from caregiving and needed a break, he traveled with me. Without him, I'd be dead myself or living as a hermit on some Oregon beach. If you're glad I'm here to write these columns, you owe your thanks to John.

As I interviewed him, I sat on our sofa, and he sat across from me in a recliner. His blond hair is long and curly. Tan, lean as a fence post, six-foot-three, he looks like a surfer. That evening, he had one leg draped over the chair's arm, a bare foot dangling. It occurred to me how much of a man he's become.

Here are excerpts from our conversation:

- John remembers the moment he realized he might lose his mom. Renee and I had spent the day at doctors' offices. John knew the physicians suspected cancer.

We'd left him money for food. Instead of buying a meal, he went to Wal-Mart for candy. He sat in our den, ate candy, played the guitar, waited. Late in the afternoon, Renee and I walked in the front door. John could see us from the den.

"I said, 'Is everything OK?'" he recalled. "You said, 'No.'"

John watched Renee and me hug in the foyer.

"She was kind of teary, and you were trying to be strong," he said.

He had been strumming a Black Crowes song, *She Talks to Angels*.

"I started playing the song, and I couldn't get through it," John said. "I put down the guitar and walked upstairs."

A few days later, I took John with me to a home repair store to buy a new commode seat. As we sat in our car in the parking lot, I explained his mom's prognosis.

"I took it in and suppressed it," he said of the awful news. "I tend to suppress everything, good and bad. I'm not a real emotional individual. Things are what they are, and we have to accept it."

- In 2001, John and I went on our first out-of-town trip together. We were frazzled. We had a conversation in our hotel room, during which John told me he'd already lost the mother he'd grown up with, and said he wished she'd go ahead and die.

"In hindsight, I kind of feel guilty for saying that," he says now. "I'm glad she didn't die right away. I'm glad I had that extra time with her."

He knew a family in which the mother got sick, and her daughter deserted her.

"I thought that was really sad," he said. "I was just really grateful I could be with my mom, and I wanted to be with her. I wanted to help take care of her, and I often felt guilty that I wasn't doing enough to help her, to help you."

- Our home always had been peaceful. A side effect of Renee's sickness was that our marriage deteriorated. She was weak. I was tired. We argued frequently.

"It stressed me out," he said. "I used to sit at the top of the steps and listen to you all fight sometimes. You kind of became Mr. Mom. I just tried to stay out of the way."

(I'm glad to say Renee and I worked out our problems long before she died. Near the end, we were as close as we'd ever been in our whole marriage.)

• Many nights after I'd gone to bed, John and Renee sat up watching TV and talking. I've always wondered what they discussed.

John said he'd grown increasingly frustrated by the silliness he saw in many Christians—people who were gratingly judgmental, or who thought they had divine answers for Renee, me or him.

"She told me I was right," he said. "A lot of times also she'd talk me down, help me relax about the situation." It comforted him to know she believed as he did.

• Watching Renee suffer made him reconsider his Christian beliefs.

"It shook them up," he said. "Now I was forced to question every-thing—if God did exist, if Jesus was really the son of God or just a good guy with a lot of good ideas. I questioned the existence of heaven and hell."

Oddly enough, he said, the classes he took at two secular state uni-versities—not church teachings—helped him the most. His college courses gave him tools for sorting "truth from myth, blind faith from real faith, fact from belief."

• Whatever the wrestling in his soul, he kept coming to church, kept playing in the worship band.

"I was glad I was there. I figured if I didn't keep going, I would lose all faith. I figured that would be as bad as having blind faith. Both ways are dangerous."

• I asked what he learned from our ordeal about Christians in general.

"That Christians are just like everyone else in the world," he said. "There are good Christians and there are bad ones."

The good ones "cared, and showed they cared. They just talked to me, and fed us. To the good Christians, the answer is always just to love."

The bad ones, he said, "were the ones who thought they had the answers for everyone. For the bad ones, the answer is always something that you're doing wrong or not doing at all."

- What is his faith like now?

"I still question, but I still believe. I wonder if I believe because I was raised to believe. But more as time goes on, I believe because I want to believe."

- John said Renee continues to be on his mind every day.

"I think about everything," he said. "It just depends on the day and my mood. I can't get the image out of my head of her dying." He remembers watching her body go into rigor mortis. "It makes me sick to my stomach, except I can't throw up."

- If he could advise other youths who have a desperately ill parent, what would he tell them?

Spend as much time as possible with your sick mom or dad, he said. "Hold onto the memories. Keep a diary, so that generations after them will know, too. That's something I didn't do, but wish I had."

- To a sick parent he would say: "Don't act angry with the kid."

One night, John and Renee had a fight. The next morning when he got up for school, he found a note of apology she'd written him while he slept.

"I still have that," he said. "It showed me that she did love me. It showed me it was hard on her, too, just being sick, but she still loved me."

- Finally, these are the truths John said he's gleaned from his experiences.

First: "I know I don't have all the answers."

Second: "It's helped me to show compassion toward others." Before, if he'd seen someone lose a parent, "I would have been like, 'So what? Get over it.'"

Now, he says, "I realize how hard it is, at any age. I both regret and am thankful for the whole situation."

MIDDLE-AGE DATING
HAS ITS UNIQUE PROS AND CONS

July 08, 2006

For the past fourteen months, I've had to consider the pros and cons of entering a relationship with some woman other than Renee, my late wife of twenty-six years.

The world appears to be full of men and women in situations similar to mine, folks who, through divorce or the death of a spouse, have been forced to start over when they'd expected to be snuggled down for the duration.

It's weird, learning to date again when you're in the throes of middle age. Dating when you're twenty is one thing. Dating when you're forty, fifty or sixty is very different.

So, for my fellow graying singles, I offer several observations.

• Don't start dating too soon—but don't wait too long. I had my first date three months after Renee died. Soon I was dating two women I'd recently met. Both were witty, educated and interesting. I liked them, and they liked me. I discovered, however, that I'd stepped out way too soon.

Even when I was with them, I thought about Renee. It wasn't fair to them. It wasn't healthy for me. So I broke off those relationships and went back to working through my grief.

On the other hand, I know people who've been single ten years and have never tried to find anyone else. That's probably a mistake, too.

We all heal at different rates. So, sure, take whatever reasonable time you need to recover—six months or three years. But don't become a hermit or a martyr.

- Don't feel guilty for moving on. I'd bring Renee back if I could, but she's dead, and nothing will change that. It's no disgrace for me or disrespect to her if I choose to walk forward. Same for you.

- Don't expect a new person to replace the one you lost. If your marriage was happy, you'll tend to measure any date against your former spouse. Don't. Remember, you had decades to build that earlier relationship. You shared a history. You had children together. You understood each other's quirks and inside jokes.

Nobody—I mean nobody—can match that immediately. Anyone new will be at a disadvantage simply because he or she is new. So concentrate on your new friend's virtues. Maybe she's more organized than your wife was. Maybe he's gentler than your first husband. Judge new flames by who they are, not by who your spouse was.

- Recognize that you might be more attractive than you think. Don't sell yourself short because you're bald or pudgy. Your rear end's broader than before, but so is your experience. Your short-term memory might not respond instantly, but your compassion does. You can't stay out all night partying, but you can afford to take your new squeeze somewhere better than McDonald's.

You can carry on meaningful conversations now because you're capable of focusing on a few topics other than sex. Some people find this appealing.

Also, keep in mind that the men or women you go out with won't look like teenage football players or cheerleaders, either. In middle age, love can't flourish if it's only skin deep.

- Accept that you can't live your life in someone else's head. Just because you're ready to date doesn't mean your children, friends or in-laws are ready to see you with someone new. They might be shocked. You need to acknowledge their feelings, but insist they respect your decisions.

- Remind yourself that there are lots of things worse than being lonesome. Never take up with someone simply because you're weary of sitting home alone watching The Weather Channel. Use discernment. If a new prospect seems stupid, narcissistic or crooked—flee.

• Don't deny your grief, but don't make an obsession of it. It's not only legitimate but productive to explain to your new romantic interest that you miss your former husband or wife. But please, after that, find something else to rattle on about. If that's all you can talk about, you shouldn't be dating yet.

• Realize that, at our age, everybody brings along some baggage. When you're eighteen, you tend to be untouched by life's harsh realities. By the time you're fifty, you've suffered. So has the person you're dating. One or both of you might have surly children, living ex-spouses, unpaid bills, psychological scars. You'll need to work through some issues together. That's OK. Take the relationship slowly.

• Celebrate your freedom. You've suffered a blow—the end of a marriage. But view this as an opportunity to explore untapped possibilities, to correct mistakes. You can do whatever you want. Singleness can be an adventure, a time to know God and yourself better, an opportunity, Lord willing, to start a new life with another person.

SUCH A REMARKABLE FRIENDSHIP IS RARE

July 22, 2006

The first night I ever spent at David Smith's house, we amused ourselves by holding a flatulence contest, which both of us thought was the funniest thing anybody had ever done, anywhere, anytime. We were in eighth grade.

We've been buddies ever since and never had an argument. I might be the only person Smith knows who he hasn't argued with. He's prickly, hard-headed, outspoken and a total non-conformist. He's also got the softest heart in thirty-four counties.

He's the only Republican in America who walks around wearing a furry Russian hat with a genuine KGB pin attached to it. He describes himself as a Marxist-Lennonist—Groucho Marx and John Lennon, that is.

In our misspent youth, we drank enough beer together to swamp an Exxon tanker ship. We thumbed our noses at the respectable world.

We chased girls together. I mainly chased. Smith mainly caught. To this day, my sister swears the teenage Smith was the most handsome guy she ever laid eyes on.

"I can get any woman I want," Smith said once. "I just can't keep any of them."

After we'd graduated from high school, his father died suddenly. Smith was in the Seabees, and I was at college. But when he arrived home on emergency leave, I was there to meet him. We drove country roads all night, reminiscing about his dad.

In my twenties, I became a Christian, quit my bad habits, then became a preacher. I thought my conversion might hurt our friendship. Smith wasn't hostile to religion in principle, but he'd never cared for Bible thumpers, either.

101

Instead, he told me, "I'm proud of you, dude."

He liked me when I was a wastrel, but he accepted me as easily when, for a spell, I turned into an overbearing zealot. He listened indulgently as I tried to save his soul.

For that matter, he liked me when I was fat and when I was fit. He never judged me. When I was broke, he bought me country ham sandwiches. When nobody else much cared for either of our company, we always enjoyed each other's.

Twenty-five years after Smith's father passed away, my wife, Renee, fell ill with cancer. I wore myself out taking care of her. Smith took me to a cabin overlooking a lake. He grilled me steaks. He told me hysterical stories, a few of which might even have been true, and made me giggle while my heart was breaking.

In the midst of Renee's long sickness, he showed up at my church one Easter so I could baptize him. It was among the more rewarding moments of my ministry.

When Renee died, Smith was at her funeral. By then, he was ailing badly himself, suffering from life-threatening health problems. But he came anyway, for my sake.

Recently, he called to say he'd taken a hard turn for the worse. He wanted to jump the broom with his girlfriend, Patricia, before it was too late to make an honest woman of her. He asked me to do the honors. It was not, to put it diplomatically, his first wedding. (A classic Smith line: "After my third marriage blew up, I had a revelation. I took a long look in the mirror and thought to myself, 'You know, maybe it's me.' Then I said, 'Nah, can't be that.'")

This time, he's found a woman who gets him. I wish he'd found her twenty years ago.

For the ceremony, held in his bride's back yard, Smith wore a garland of hand-woven flowers in his bushy salt-and-pepper hair, a tie-dyed T-shirt, buckskin hunting pants and suede bedroom slippers—an outfit he called "Dave's tux."

True to his old form, after the "I do's" were finished, he danced with several women—at once. He flirted with my date.

102

I took him a wedding present—a military medal I'd ordered from eBay. As the assembled well-wishers looked on, I read the citation:

"Let it be known that from March 1956 until the present, David Lee Smith II repeatedly has displayed gallantry above and beyond the call of duty. Through guerrilla warfare, clandestine operations and open battle, Smith, against all odds and often at great danger to his personal safety, has single-handedly challenged idiots, jerks, nabobs, cretins, muckety-mucks, self-appointed grand pooh-bahs, nincompoops, gasbags, Republicans, Democrats, Rotarians and hypocrites. Employing as his weapons stealth, stinging wit and occasional stupidity, Smith has punctured countless balloons and fatally wounded all sacred cows."

When it came time for me to leave, he hugged me tightly. Then he gave me three exaggerated pats on the back.

"You know what the three pats mean," he said. "I'm—not—gay."

As my date and I drove away, I must have fallen silent, because she asked me what I was thinking.

"I was thinking," I said, "that I can't imagine a world without Smith in it."

I'm not embarrassed to tell you that I love the guy.

NO LABEL FITS ALL

September 23, 2006

Chris Rock said it in one of his comedy routines: Nobody is just one thing. It's a marvelous, common-sense observation we forget constantly.

The more I listen to the political and religious discourse in this country, the more I want to blast Rock's routine from loudspeakers on every courthouse square.

As a culture, we tend to label people and dump them into broad categories. We call them liberals, fundamentalists, Catholics, Jews, gays, rednecks, blacks, whites, Muslims, skinheads, Goths, the media—and having done so, we feel comfortable in dismissing them, assuming we know all their habits, tastes and opinions.

Perhaps it's always been this way. In a used-book store, I stumbled across *The Tyranny of Words* by Stuart Chase, an economist and an adviser to Franklin Roosevelt.

Chase had noticed an identical tendency in his day. He argued that stupid governmental policies and even wars often result from our generalizing about people we call simply "Germans," "Communists" or "the poor."

The truth is, individual humans are endlessly complicated and contradictory. They defy a single classification. And any political movement, geographical region, economic system or religious sect made up of 1,000 or 100 million humans is 1,000 or 100 million times more complex and contradictory than its individual members.

Labels are just that: labels. They're shorthand. They're abbreviations.

They're sometimes necessary. In a speech or a TV newscast, you can't identify by name and describe in detail every one of the Earth's 1.1 billion Roman Catholics.

But rarely are labels accurate, either. Rarely are they healthy.

Too often, they allow us to justify our own sloppy thinking and prejudices.

You could easily classify me according to any one of a slew of labels. I'm male. I'm middle-aged. I'm straight. I'm a small-town Kentuckian. I'm a Pentecostal preacher.

Those descriptions probably conjure up for some folks a whole wheelbarrow load of assumptions about me. Many of those assumptions would be mistaken.

I enjoy going to art galleries, independent movies and museums. My favorite TV shows are *The Sopranos, The Simpsons, Da Ali G Show* and *Curb Your Enthusiasm*. I have three college degrees. I've traveled widely, and I'm about as comfortable in San Francisco or New York City as in Mount Sterling.

I love boxing and football—you're on the money if you guessed that—but I've never even seen a NASCAR race.

I've voted for Democrats and Republicans about equally.

On the First Amendment, I'm as liberal as it gets. I believe anybody should be allowed to read, watch, write or say any loony thing he danged well pleases. I think the state should keep its nose out of religion, and the church should stay out of politics.

On the Second Amendment, I'm conservative. I neither collect guns nor hunt, but I learned to shoot a rifle and pistol before I learned to read, and I say let the good ol' boys (how's that for a label?) keep their ballistic toys.

As for the Third Amendment, I'm for it. It prohibits the government from quartering soldiers in civilian homes during peacetime. It's a good rule, but I can't tell whether agreeing with it is a liberal or conservative position.

Now, if you can describe all that with one word, I'd like to see it.

The labels we attach to other people are equally as incomplete. I know grandmas who have tattoos and pierced navels instead of blue hair and tear-drop eyeglasses. I know black guys who drive pickups, chew tobacco and listen to country music. I know white, middle-class kids who wear their pants around their thighs, stick their baseball caps on sideways and listen to hip-hop. I know evangelical Christians who cuss like mule skinners. I've met conservative Republicans who are as gay as Liberace.

Speaking of gay people, is anyone gay and that's all? Even if some particular gay guy happens to be so hormonally wrought up that he spends, let's say, two hours every single day pursuing his sexuality, that also means he spends twenty-two hours doing other things. More than ninety percent of the time he's something else, maybe a Cats fan, a computer programmer, a customer at Wal-Mart, a brother, a friend, a tenant. He's not just gay.

I used to have an image in my mind, a label, of what an Iraqi was. But then we invaded Iraq, and, in the aftermath, I've learned there are Kurdish Iraqis, Sunni Iraqis, Shiite Iraqis and Christian Iraqis. Some Iraqis admire Saddam Hussein. Some hate him. Some Iraqis love Americans. Some want to kill us. I'd bet most Iraqis only want to eat well and walk safe streets, that they couldn't care less about the politics of it. Just like us.

As Chase would have put it, there's no such thing as "The Iraqis." There's only Iraqi1, Iraqi2, Iraqi3 ... all the way up to Iraqi25,000,000. They're all unique.

As I said, we can't always avoid using labels. But we should always keep in mind that they are, by their nature, inaccurate. And they're terribly easy to abuse.

BLAME WORLD'S TROUBLES ON A GENE

December 09, 2006

I've long believed that many of the religious and even cultural battles waged today really aren't about Christianity, Islam, Judaism or, for that matter, secularism.

They're about two competing mindsets that transcend any specific faith group: extremism versus moderation.

A friend told me about a dinner she shared with a couple in another state, the male half of whom was raised a Muslim in Egypt.

My friend grew up in rural Kentucky, where she and her family were members of an unusually strict Christian sect. Over supper, she and her Egyptian-American acquaintance compared notes about their religious heritages.

She told him about the warnings she'd heard from her church's elders that members of their group would be the only ones going to heaven, about the elders' literal—and, in her opinion, selective—interpretation of the Bible, about the inflexible, frequently petty rules that governed members' private behavior.

Repeatedly, she said, her companion looked at her in astonishment and exclaimed, "Me, too! This is exactly like extremist Islam!"

The two had been born on opposite sides of the earth, into faiths their adherents would consider antithetical. One group trusted in Jesus, and the other in Allah. But the worldviews were identical.

My friend's story didn't surprise me.

I've seen extremist Christians, Muslims and Jews—and extremist Marxists, feminists and environmentalists.

107

My pet theory is that there's an extremist gene that drives a certain percentage of people in every society, just as some folks have biological predispositions toward intelligence, heart disease or tallness.

I predict that one day scientists will isolate this gene. They'll find it blocks its carriers from perceiving philosophical grays, much less a full-color spectrum.

These people have, in effect, spiritual color-blindness. They see everything in stark blacks and whites. I'm not sure they can help it.

There are variations from person to person and from sect to sect, but generally their world looks like this:

- Our group is good; therefore, all other groups are evil.
- Our holy book is true; thus, all other holy books are lies.
- God is exclusively on our side; therefore, anyone who disagrees with us is disagreeing not with us but with God Almighty.
- We're a minority, surrounded by sinners conspiring against us; therefore, we must shun or—in extreme cases—kill those who aren't like us.
- People who believe as we do once ruled society, and in those days, the world was blissful; therefore, we must rule again.

Ironically, extremists don't just loathe heathens or liberals; they loathe competing extremists, too. In Iraq, extremist Sunni Muslims and extremist Shiite Muslims slaughter one another daily. During the Reformation and Counter-Reformation, zealous Protestants and Catholics murdered one another with an equal self-righteousness.

The fallacies inherent in extremist assumptions should be obvious—and are obvious to those of us who don't share that predisposition.

For instance, a given extremist group might indeed be good. I was raised in a conservative Christian denomination and experienced firsthand its many virtues.

But for me, it never naturally followed that everyone outside our church was bad. I played sports with Methodists, Catholics and even the occasional agnostic. I saw them in the locker room and noticed they hadn't sprouted cloven hooves or pointy tails.

Today, I still believe strongly in the truth of the Christian Bible. But that doesn't of itself mean the sacred books of Jews or Muslims are without any merit.

And I've learned that no matter what I believe, most people—even those who think I'm nuts, and there are a lot of those—aren't conspiring against me. Most folks tend their business and are content to let me tend mine. The planet doesn't revolve around me.

Sadly, it's nearly impossible for people from these two worldviews—moderation and extremism—to establish anything resembling an open, two-way conversation.

For extremists, any acknowledgment that their path might not be the only path endangers their souls; such an admission amounts to heresy. It's a trick of Satan.

Their theology is driven not by grace, but by fear: of incurring God's wrath, of entertaining facts that contradict what they believe, of losing their faith.

Probably the best we can hope for, then, is what we have now in this country: an uneasy mutual toleration. I hope this toleration, at least, endures.

BEING A LIBERAL ISN'T SO BAD—
BUT I'M NOT ONE

January 13, 2007

I'm occasionally asked whether I'm a liberal.

Liberal is a nebulous term. It means different things to different people in different contexts.

When I eat at my favorite Italian restaurant, I might say afterward that the cook was liberal with the meatballs. I mean it as a compliment. I'm pointing out that the cook was generous, that he gave me more food than I'd expected.

In that sense, I hope I am liberal: I hope I'm generous and kind-hearted.

But typically when people toss the L-word in my direction, they don't intend it as a compliment. They say it with a snarl, a glare, a dismissive jerk of the chin: "Oh, what are you, some kind of (sniff) LIB-er-al?"

They're questioning my views on hot-button social or religious topics.

So, addressing that sense of the word, allow me to go on record. Imagine my left hand—so to speak—on a Bible, my right hand raised in a solemn vow.

No sir, Senator, I'm not now, nor have I ever been, a bona fide member of the liberal persuasion. As I've said before, I'm liberal on a few issues, conservative on a few, but mainly an incurable middle-of-the-roader.

Still, if I were a liberal, I wouldn't be ashamed of it.

We seem to forget that virtually every political and religious break-through we now take for granted was, in its time, considered liberal, blasphemous, pinko, wacko.

Here's a short list of liberals and their batty ideas:

- Jesus was a liberal. He challenged the status quo, the ruling elite, at every turn. He fed the masses for free. He worked on the Sabbath. He dined with tax cheats and hookers while poking fun at the hyper-religious Sadducees and Pharisees. He preferred the sick and outcast to the rich. The establishment killed him for such supposed sins.

- John Wycliffe was a liberal reformer. He thought the church should be stripped of all its wealth and political influence. He wanted religious leadership placed in the hands of "poor priests" who would be bound by no formal creeds. To these ends, he helped produce the first English translation of the New Testament, so common people such as you and I could read the Bible for ourselves. He was persecuted as a heretic.

- The Founding Fathers were liberals. In fact, they were revolutionaries, which is why their war is called the Revolutionary War. Their beliefs in, among other things, free speech, a free press and freedom of religion were truly radical.

- In the mid-1800s, those who wanted to abolish slavery were specifically labeled radicals by their opponents. Conservatives thought the owning of slaves was a God-given right. We fought a civil war over that one.

- Until less than a century ago, evangelical Christianity ranked among the more politically liberal of church movements. Evangelicals championed everything from abolition to free universal education to the fair treatment of Indians—and, for their efforts, were dismissed as subversive bleeding hearts.

- Those who promoted women's suffrage were liberals.

- Virtually all the civil rights leaders of the 1950s and 1960s were decried as liberals—and even as traitors to the American way.

- The people who protested the Vietnam War were liberals.

- In the 1970s, those who thought women should be able to work outside the home and earn wages equal to those paid to men were liberals.

- Ad infinitum.

If you love Jesus, if you're blessed to read his words in English, if you enjoy living in a country where you can preach any fool thing you want to, if you're happy that slavery is illegal, if you've benefited from public schools, if you're relieved that women can vote, if you're glad black people share full rights as citizens, if you're sorry we lost 58,000 men in Vietnam but grateful we didn't lose more, if you think it's fair that one half of the population is eligible to earn as much as the other half—then thank a liberal.

Which isn't to say that liberals never promote bad causes. Communism, to cite one example, was a liberal idea. We all know what happened there.

Eventually, though, most liberal campaigns become society's accepted wisdom. A generation or two late, the very types of folks who initially opposed liberal innovations embrace them as obvious truths—and pretend they thought them up.

I don't even agree with the terms "liberal" and "conservative." I'd prefer saying "early adapter" and "late adapter."

Anyway, no—I wouldn't classify myself as a liberal. But the liberals' record is, by and large, excellent. Their instincts usually are aimed in the proper direction. Liberals want to expand our liberties, to help the dispossessed. When it comes to the big issues, we often discover, if only in retrospect, that the left was right.

OK, GOD HAS NO GENDER,
BUT I STILL USE 'HE'

March 10, 2007

Occasionally, readers ask why I continue the archaic practice of referring to God as "he."

The answer: Because he told me to. (No, no, that's a joke!)

Many Christian scholars, ministers and lay members are troubled by the consistent use of masculine terms in old church texts and, traditionally, from pulpits.

Newer translations of the Bible, and prayer book and hymnal revisions as well, tend to employ fewer gender-specific words for God and for Christians.

For instance, in the King James Bible, St. Paul begins his second letter to the church at Thessalonica like this, "We are bound to thank God always for you, brethren."

In the more recent New Living Translation, the passage is rendered, "Dear brothers and sisters, we always thank God for you."

I have no problem with using such inclusive language in religious texts when it refers to the children of Israel, members of the early church or humanity in general.

I'm not an authority on, say, ancient Greek, the language in which the New Testament was written. As best I can understand, though, Greek writers, when addressing groups, frequently used masculine terminology to indicate both sexes.

The New Testament's authors clearly were, in most cases, writing to the whole membership of churches: men and women, free people and slaves, Romans and Jews.

113

To me, however, when we refer to a singular God, masculine images such as "father" and pronouns such as "his" remain preferable.

I realize that God transcends gender altogether. God isn't a man. He isn't confined to any kind of tangible body. God is a spirit.

As early as Genesis, the scriptures tell us that people were created in God's image—as men and women. I take that to mean God possesses attributes of both sexes. Or, I should say, both sexes possess God's attributes.

Still, I prefer to call God "he" for several reasons:

- I'm a writer. Perhaps you can't tell it from my columns, but I try to express myself as gracefully as my limited talent allows.

From an aesthetic standpoint, the gender-neutral language some modernists adopt makes me want to run screaming from the room.

I took a seminary class in New Testament studies. To avoid calling God "he," the professor would say things such as: "God says about Godself that God's nature is love."

Godself? Three repetitions of "God" in one short sentence?

Years later, I'm still cringing.

- I'm not comfortable calling God "she," much less "it."

"It" denotes an inanimate object such as a table, or a beast such as a cow. That won't work. I'm not at ease calling God "she," either. That's not because I have anything against women. And, as I said, God possesses as many female characteristics as male.

Nonetheless, Christians have called God "he" for 2,000 years.

That, in itself, neither makes the practice right nor wrong. But a lot of times, even in 2007, folks who refer to God as "she" do so mainly for shock value. I suspect that far more of my readers, men and women, are happier with the traditional "he."

If I were to write, "God says about herself that her nature is love," the column instantly would quit being about God's love. It would suddenly be about God's gender, about politics, about everything but love.

- Finally, I believe that nearly all the biblical figures, from the Hebrew prophets to Jesus and the apostles, made conscious decisions to depict the Judeo-Christian God using male images.

Lots of folks argue that this is because the Bible's heroes and authors were men, and thus biased. The issue isn't quite that simple. The New Testament's writers, for example, lived within in a larger culture dominated by Greek and Roman religions. If anything, Greco-Roman society was more misogynistic than early Christian society. Yet Greeks and Romans regularly worshiped female deities.

I think the Christian writers were making an intentional statement.

Something about what they understood as God's revelation to them led them to identify their God as male. In doing so, they were going against the cultural grain.

Most telling is that in every record we have of Jesus' teachings, he describes God as a father, not as a mother, as male rather than female. I decline to overrule Jesus.

That said, other people can do what they want. Honestly, I'm not offended.

And I intend no offense. But until further notice, I'll go on calling God "he," as I've always done. I find that imperfect, yet more fluid, less confrontational and more scriptural than the alternatives.

THERE ARE NO CHRISTIANS
WITHOUT FLAWS

April 28, 2007

I've often wondered how different—and how much healthier—religion might be if the people who practice it felt free to be honest. About everything.

On April 19, Mary Winkler, age thirty-three, was convicted of voluntary manslaughter for the 2006 shotgun slaying of her husband, Matthew. The minister at Fourth Street Church of Christ in Selmer, Tenn., Matthew, age thirty-one, was regarded by his congregation as a moral, God-fearing man.

That is, until Mary killed him. Her trial revealed a man and a marriage at odds with others' perceptions. According to her, the Winklers lived in hell, their home life wracked by financial turmoil, physical abuse and sexual perversion.

What struck me most about this story was that, invariably, when members of the Winklers' church were questioned by reporters, they seemed bewildered.

The Winklers, they said, appeared to be the model Christian couple: pleasant, devoted to each other, sincere in their faith.

I don't want to make too broad a point from a sensationalistic news story or from the testimony of a defendant trying to exonerate herself.

But one thing is clear: the couple had huge problems of some kind. You don't blast your mate with a shotgun unless there are issues in your relationship.

I suspect what may have kept the Winklers from seeking the help they needed was a pressure applied to churchgoers generally, and clergy in particular, to pretend they've got it all together.

Which, of course, is a lie of cosmic proportions.

Nobody's got it all together. Everybody has flaws, sins and troubles. Everybody.

Yet people scrub their flesh and put on their Sunday best and drive to church and divinely sing hymns even when their hearts are ripped to shreds. They feel compelled to act as if nothing's wrong. They're terrified that if they admit their failures, they'll be branded as bad Christians.

Too often, they're right.

A genuine pathology operates in many, if not most, religious organizations.

Recently, I spoke to a group of folks in a program that trains pastors, church counselors and hospice chaplains.

In the question-and-answer session that followed my talk, we somehow got off on a sad fact: Whenever a crisis strikes a congregation—a beloved teenager dies in a car wreck, a dispute arises over doctrine, an elder gets a messy divorce—it's usually the members who beforehand seemed the most spiritual who respond the worst.

They're the first to descend into fury, condemnation, faction-forming and finger-pointing. Or else they just disappear.

I said I'd witnessed this phenomenon, but had no explanation for it.

Afterward, as he walked me to my car, one of the program's directors told me he could offer an answer.

"I'm all ears," I said. "Enlighten me. This ranks among life's great mysteries."

He said research suggests that people who are ostentatiously, often legalistically, religious share the same personality profiles as alcoholics and addicts.

You know who he was talking about. They're perfectly sane, but can't cheer for their favorite ball team without working a Bible verse into their rah-rahs. They claim to receive direct messages from the Lord every fifteen minutes. They're always aggrieved at the waywardness of other Christians; hardly anyone is righteous enough to suit them.

Basically, my host said, these folks tend to use their faith in the same ways, and for the same reasons, that crackheads use the pipe.

They've got untreated emotional wounds they can't deal with. Religion becomes their anesthetic. It wards off the pain of, say, a fractured family or riddled self-esteem.

When a new problem threatens to cut through this anesthetic haze, they perceive it as an attack on their fragile well-being. If God didn't protect their fellow churchgoer's child, maybe God won't protect their child either. So, out of self-defense, they latch onto some supposed sin the child's mother committed and blame his death on that.

His explanation made perfect sense.

You find these people in almost every congregation, sometimes in prominent positions. They create a circle of dysfunction. They won't address their real issues—and they intimidate others from admitting their own fears, hurts and shortcomings.

Ministers are even more cowed by these people than their parishioners are. God help the pastor who shows them any hint of doubt or weakness.

I didn't know the Winklers. I don't know where Selmer, Tenn., is. But I'm pretty sure nobody ever told that poor couple it's OK to be messed up. Being believers shouldn't require us to deny our failings. It should lead us to confess them.

If you're screwed up (and you are), admit it straight out. Honest and similarly flawed folks will rush to help. You'll be astounded at the kindred souls you discover.

As for the prigs—let them howl. After all, they're not really howling. They're only whistling in the dark.

MY SHAVED HEAD
IS A SIGHT TO BEHOLD

July 28, 2007

Last week, I had my brother-in-law, Tracy, shaved my head bald as a cue ball.

The downside is, my girlfriend says I look like, as she tactfully phrased it, "a redneck skinhead sociopath."

The upside is, people have quit cutting me off in traffic. They glance at me behind the wheel of my car, then give me a wide, wide berth.

Some guys look suave with their heads shaved. I'm not one of those guys.

But I didn't do this to repulse my girlfriend or intimidate strangers.

I did it to support my sister, Cathi. At forty-five, she's been diagnosed with breast cancer. She's already endured a double mastectomy and begun what's scheduled to be six months of chemotherapy.

I decided if she was going bald, I'd go bald with her. Tracy and my son, John, also cut off their hair.

Life takes bizarre twists. My immediate family used to include three women: my wife, my mom and Cathi.

Cathi's the only one left.

And now she's got breast cancer.

What's even weirder is that none of these women were related biologically. Our folks adopted Cathi when she was a newborn.

Figure the odds. Three women, no genetic link, three cases of breast cancer.

Thank God, it seems Cathi will be with us a long time. Doctors found her disease early, and it hadn't spread. Her prognosis is excellent.

Still, I've had her on my mind pretty much every waking moment.

When she and I were kids, we could barely tolerate each other. I'd been an only child for six years before she came along, and her arrival disturbed my equilibrium.

From the beginning, she was voluble, willful and impulsive. I was quiet, obedient and methodical. As soon as she could walk, she wanted to follow me everywhere. I tried every trick I could think of to get away from her.

We blended about as well as butterscotch pudding and pickle juice.

Then something fortunate happened. We grew up. We became friends.

Cathi is a scream. She'll say anything, to anybody (little of which I can repeat in a family newspaper). Someone told me recently that Cathi and I are the only two people on Earth who find cancer funny. Lately, we share a lot of jokes about boobs.

She teaches special education. Her school kids adore her. She's a middle-age, middle-class white woman who knows every rap song ever recorded.

A few years ago, one of her teenage students became especially attached to Cathi. Lorrie had been abused. She'd grown up in foster care and group homes. Her one desire was to have a real family.

So Cathi and Tracy moved her into their house and became the parents she'd longed for. Lorrie's married now, but visits constantly and still calls them Mom and Dad.

Tracy's a story in himself. He was raised in the mountains under bad circumstances. In fact, at six-foot-seven and almost 300 pounds, he is a mountain. He's been a professional wrestler, a jail guard and a cop. He's tattooed. He's hardcore tough.

Yet he worships Cathi. Now that she's sick, he won't leave her side. Literally.

Back in 2003, when our mom was dying, both Cathi and Tracy sat in the hospital with her around the clock, for days on end.

Since then, they've been the main companions to our father, who's getting on in years. They're buying a house across the street from him, to be even nearer.

I not only love Cathi, but I owe her a lot.

So, if you happen to see me anytime soon, I look like a Grade A doofus.

A shaved head does not become me.

But it was the least I could do. Basically, it was all I could do.

LESSONS FROM MY
IMAGINARY SEMINARY

August 11, 2007

Sorting through old columns, I found that in 2002 I wrote a piece about what I'd learned during my twenty years as a pastor—the insights I'd pass on to younger ministers if they were to ask me.

Not that anyone actually had asked me. Not that anyone's asked me now.

Nevertheless, as I reread that column, it hit me I've reached the twenty-five-year mark—a quarter of a century in the pulpit. That itself gave me pause. But I also was struck that my ministerial priorities today aren't quite the same as they were even half a decade ago.

I've never considered myself a successful pastor, if you measure success by a large congregation or public acclaim. What I have been, I hope, is faithful.

And, as I observed five years ago, if you do anything faithfully for a long time, whether it's laying bricks or preaching sermons, you learn a few things.

If I ran my own private little seminary, here's what I'd teach aspiring clergy:

• Meaningful religion is about relationships, not rules. The longer I attempt, in my own messed-up way, to serve God, the more I suspect he couldn't care less whether we let slip an occasional four-letter word or forget to bless our hamburgers.

What matters is that we pause regularly to thank him for his mercy, that we wait to hear whether he's whispering to us, and that we bestow a mercy similar to God's on the clerk whose cash register has jammed and held up our line.

122

- Often, the best thing we can say is nothing. We ministers feel compelled to furnish all the answers. Well, we don't have all the answers and, even if we did, people in excruciating pain are in no condition to receive those answers.

Don't rush up to a parishioner who's just lost both her parents in a house fire and tell her that God is good, all the time. Don't tell her heaven needed two more angels. Don't spout Scripture.

Just show up. Say, "I am so, so sorry." Then sit down and keep your mouth shut. Stay a while. That's the greatest witness of all. It's called the ministry of presence.

- It's easy to dismiss other people's views—until we get to know the people. Nobody forms his or her faith in a vacuum. People do what they do for a reason. They believe what they believe for a reason.

I've heard Catholics and Episcopalians put down Pentecostals for speaking in tongues or getting emotional. I've heard Pentecostals jeer at Catholics and Episcopalians for wearing brightly colored robes in church or drinking martinis after services.

Fortunately, I've been blessed to worship with each of those groups—and with many more besides. I've found a lot of gracious, sincere believers (and a few absolute idiots) in every group. God works his will in different ways through different people. God didn't give your sect the only revelation he's got. Accept it. Get over yourself.

- We're not as holy as we think we are, much less as holy as others want us to be. We're sinners at heart, even if we snap on a collar and get paid to expound divine truths. Given the wrong set of circumstances, you and I will behave very badly. It's wise to keep this in mind. It helps us stay humble, which we ought to be.

- God is mysterious, and smarter than we are. We'll never figure him out. As embarrassing as I sometimes find it to reread my old newspaper columns, I find it even more painful to go back and reread old journals and sermon notes.

I went through a period when I preached that the Second Coming of Jesus was sure to occur any minute. I went through another period when I thought my church, Kentucky and the whole country were about to experience a massive revival on the scale of The Second Great Awakening in the early 1800s.

I had my theories. God had other plans.

- Here's a point I made in 2002, and still hold to be central: Even for ministers, the gospel is the simplest message on Earth. It boils down to principles a kindergartner could understand: Love them all and forgive them all; if we do that, God will love and forgive us. It's simple, but not easy. We should try to always be motivated by love. We won't always succeed, but we should try. Whether we're dealing with an infidel who opposes our faith or a deacon who's siphoned cash from the plate, we should seek what's truly best for him.

As I said, these aren't, for the most part, the same points I made five years ago.

Which just goes to show you ... something. I'm not sure what.

Oh, yeah: Faith is a journey. And you can quote me on that.

CARE AND FEEDING OF THE PASTOR

August 25, 2007

In my last column, I wrote about what I've learned during twenty-five years as a pastor, and listed several lessons I'd teach younger clergy if I ran my own private seminary.

That prompted an e-mail from a reader who urged me to talk about another similar issue, the advice he thought experienced ministers ought to impart to lay people.

I've written on that topic before. But the points my correspondent made are better than mine. Unfortunately, he asked that I not identify him, other than to describe him as the son and brother of preachers.

Here's what he suggested:

Rule No. 1: If you don't like the pastor of the church you're attending, don't look around for like-minded folks to try to run the pastor out of the church. Just leave. Also (this ought to be obvious) don't spread lies about the pastor to help gather support for ousting the pastor.

Rule No. 2: If you don't agree with what the pastor says from the pulpit, don't call him at home an hour later while he's eating dinner with his family. Wait until the pastor has office hours.

Rule No. 3: Don't expect the pastor to feel the same outrage you do about a certain sin. You can ask him to address that sin, but if he isn't as wrought up about it as you are, understand that pastors are as different in their feelings as regular people.

Rule No. 4: Before you become a churchgoer, ask yourself whether you have it in you to forgive others. God forgives us and wants us to be forgiving. If you don't have the capacity to do that, you might not be ready to join a church.

Rule No. 5: Don't tell the pastor after a sermon that his message made you feel down. Don't tell him your reason for coming to church is to feel good. If you read the Bible, which many preachers base their sermons on, you'll find there's a lot of bad stuff in there. And sometimes the truth hurts.

Rule No. 6: Don't have unrealistic expectations for the pastor to visit the sick members of your church. If a pastor visits a sick person three times, some people will complain he should have visited four times.

Rule No. 7: Keep in mind that churches, and the world, would be better off if each person worked on improving himself, instead of trying to work on others.

These rules come nearly verbatim from my publicity-shy correspondent.

Now, let me add Paul's corollaries:

Corollary No. 1: Don't complain about the church's tattered carpet, tinny sound system or part-time pastor if you're not contributing generously to help provide new carpet, a better sound system or a full-time salary.

Corollary No. 2: Not only should you not spread gossip about the pastor, don't listen to such gossip. At the first hint someone's about to tell tales, say, "Wait, let me get my pen, so I can jot this down. I'll want to run it by the minister and get her side of the story, too. I'll be sure to tell her where I heard it, so she'll know who to see if she needs to correct any untruths."

Corollary No. 3: Don't judge the minister's performance too hastily. No job is as easy from the inside as it looks from the outside. You have no idea why the pastor makes some of the decisions he does. He hears confidential confessions he can't disclose to you. He knows more about internal church politics and personalities than you do.

Addendum to Corollary No. 3: If you wouldn't want the preacher to spend her weekdays standing around your accounting office telling you how to be a more effective CPA, don't hang around the church telling her how to be a better pastor.

126

Corollary No. 4: Keep in mind you're not the only person in the congregation; not every sermon, pleasant or unpleasant, is meant for you. Not every new program the church starts will meet your individual needs. There are 50 or 500 other people involved. Think back to what you learned in first grade: Sometimes it's the other person's turn.

In closing, I hasten to add that the finest people I've ever met are lay members of the congregation I serve. But along the way, like every other minister, I've run into a few Christians more diabolical than old Slewfoot himself.

Whatever house of worship you attend, make it your goal to be that former type of parishioner, not the latter.

JUST LIKE MOTHER TERESA, I DOUBTED

September 08, 2007

According to the August 23rd issue of *Time*, a new collection of Mother Teresa's correspondence, *Mother Teresa: Come Be My Light*, reveals in detail a startling dimension of her private life.

During most of her ministry among the dying on Calcutta's streets and her ascent to international fame, Mother Teresa doubted God's very existence. She felt no hint of Christ's presence in her heart. Repeatedly, her letters show, she poured out her frustration to priests. She refers to her ongoing spiritual condition as "dryness," "darkness," "loneliness" and "torture." She confesses in one letter, "I no longer pray."

Time's article includes the predictable, and understandable, charge by critics that Mother Teresa's letters prove her to have been a fraud. With equal predictability, her admirers rush to defend her. I'd fall into that group.

To me, whatever her misgivings, perhaps because of her misgivings, Mother Teresa embodied *agape*, a Greek term the New Testament's writers use to describe Christian love. Agape is a unique word. It implies a love much different than, say, romantic love, which tends to depend on our feelings of affection.

By definition, agape isn't primarily the product of our emotions, but of our will. We choose to perform loving acts even when we might not feel loving. Agape is about what we actually do, not what we think about what we do or those we do it for.

Mother Teresa continued to serve God even though she felt little affection for him. She rescued the sick even as her soul, in her words, remained an "ice block."

I suspect Mother Teresa suffered from compassion fatigue, a psychological condition common to medical workers and family caregivers.

Compassion fatigue strikes when you've given and given of yourself until you're given out. You've exhausted your spiritual reserves. You've ached until you're numb. Physically, you're still going through the motions, but emotionally, your heart is barren.

It's at this point that God often seems the most coldly distant: when we're the most desperate for his warming presence. We beg, we promise, we cry—he says nothing. Or, if he is talking, we've lost our ability to hear him.

My own experiences pale in comparison with Mother Teresa's. But I do know about compassion fatigue. During the five years I nursed my dying wife, I prayed every day for some answer from God, a sign of his presence, no matter how meager. I didn't need a blinding flash of light. A whispered word, even a pat on the shoulder, metaphysically speaking, would have been plenty.

I got nothing. For a long time, I felt no love from God, and thus, gradually, I came to feel little love for God. I wasn't sure God existed. I didn't love myself anymore, and because of that I wondered whether I loved anyone else. (Jesus told us to love our neighbors as ourselves, but if you despise yourself, it's hard to care about your neighbor.)

Now I see another side to what we endured.

I've watched the Lord employ our family's trials toward a greater end. I've written about our ordeals, and in return received innumerable grateful e-mails, calls and letters from sick people and caregivers who are suffering through similar difficulties.

I'm invited to speak to hospice groups, churches and colleges about these matters.

And I find that my faith—battered as it was—seems to have recovered.

To be sure, it's different now. I'm different. But I do have faith again.

Today I think, "Maybe God was there all along. Maybe he had a purpose in all that. Even in his silence, perhaps there was a plan."

If nothing else, my own emptiness, my seeming abandonment, taught me how weak and lost I am. I found out I can't do it alone. I need God. Desperately.

But there was an end to my trials. I've had time to recuperate. I've gained the benefits of distance and hindsight.

Mother Teresa's work among the dying never relented. I helped take care of two sick people over a half-decade. She took care of thousands over a half-century.

To me, her despair makes her not less of a saint than I thought she was, but more of one. Her letters prove that even the greatest believers struggle, that, to even the most anointed, God may seem absent, not just occasionally, but continually.

Still, she plodded on, changing soiled bedclothes, applying bandages to the putrefied wounds of the dying. She was, as St. Paul put it, constant in season and out.

We should learn from her. When the master seems to have moved overseas and left no forwarding address, we ought to keep stumbling forward, doing the work he's called us to. For sooner or later, he'll return. Sooner or later, he always returns.

In this world or the next, we'll meet him again. And when we do, we want to hear him say, "Well done, good and faithful servant."

FROM ONE NAUGHTY BOY TO ANOTHER

September 22, 2007

Earlier this month, CNN talk-show host Larry King tossed former President Bill Clinton a lob: What do you think about Idaho Sen. Larry Craig's difficulties?

Clinton's response was amazing.

Craig, a Republican, ranked among Clinton's harshest critics during Clinton's 1999 Senate impeachment trial, which resulted largely from his affair with White House intern Monica Lewinsky.

Craig once described Clinton as "a nasty, bad, naughty boy," *New Yorker* writer Hendrik Hertzberg recalled in a recent magazine piece.

In a classic example of "what goes around comes around," it has emerged that Craig, an outspoken political and moral conservative, was arrested in June in a Minneapolis-St. Paul International Airport public restroom for allegedly soliciting sex from a male undercover police officer. Craig pleaded guilty to disorderly conduct.

When news of his *faux pas* became public, he claimed he actually wasn't guilty, that his arrest had amounted to a misunderstanding between him and the cop.

He'd entered his plea, he said, because he was stressed over an Idaho newspaper's persecution of him. The newspaper, oddly enough, had raised questions about Craig's sexual orientation.

It's a weird coincidence, that an Idaho newspaper would question Craig's heterosexuality—and that, hundreds of miles and several states away, an airport cop would then charge him with seeking random sex in a men's bathroom.

131

By the time King's interview with Clinton aired on September 5, even Craig's fellow Republicans were lined up at their podiums to disown him.

So King tossed Clinton, a Democrat, that aforementioned lob.

If Clinton had taken the opportunity to gloat, who could have blamed him?

Here's Craig, who attacked him unmercifully, now busted for misconduct many Americans would consider even more embarrassing than Clinton's.

Instead, to my eyes, Clinton looked genuinely sad. He replied that he "didn't feel any great joy" about Craig's predicament. He understood what it was like to be humiliated and ridiculed for your weaknesses:

"I just know right now he and his family have got to be hurting," Clinton said, "and I think the rest of us should just be pulling for their personal lives, and the politics of this will play itself out."

When King pressed him, Clinton said he'd learned from his own scandal:

"One of the things I did to get through that was to think hard about times in my past, when I had judged people too harshly because they had a problem I didn't have. And I promised myself I'd never do that again, and I'm trying to keep that promise."

King asked why so often those who bray the loudest against other people's sins turn out to be every bit as wretched as the folks they're condemning.

"I think maybe it's subconscious self-hatred, I don't know," Clinton said. "Maybe it's a desire to avoid being caught. Maybe it's just a desire to deal with what they perceive to be the social and political realities they find themselves in."

Clinton's generosity of spirit dumbfounded me.

Still, we should note that he chose to speak so humanely of Craig because Clinton now recognizes from harsh experience his own humanity. By his own admission, he, too, once wagged his finger at people who messed up and fell from grace.

Until he messed up and fell from grace.

Sad to say, that's how we learn compassion—by finding ourselves in dire need of it. The central fact of human existence is that we're all knotheads, every last one of us.

Life has a way of coming back to slap us in the face.

Do you hate gay people?

Guess what. You're going to end up with a gay son or a wife who decides after twenty years of marriage she's a lesbian. You're going to find yourself lying in an intensive care unit where your doctor, the person you pray can keep you alive, is gay.

Do you deplore the way other people raise their children?

Look out. One of your children will become a crackhead.

Do you loathe adulterers?

You'll find yourself in a bad spot in your own marriage, sitting next to a comely co-worker you can't resist.

Do you think alcoholics are weak-willed losers?

You're going to end up addicted to Twinkies and weighing 350 pounds.

The best approach is to treat sinners gently, the way you'd like to be treated if you were in their shoes. Because sooner or later, you will be in their shoes.

HERE ARE SOME GIFTS
MINISTERS WOULD LIKE

October 13, 2007

Sunday is Clergy Appreciation Day, and my editor suggested I set forth some ways congregations might show their gratitude to their ministers.

Never one to pass up an opportunity to solicit graft for myself (I am, after all, a pastor), I readily agreed.

Here are tips for letting your spiritual leaders know how much they mean to you:

- Paste a picture of the pastor's head over a life-size cutout of Brad Pitt's body, and stand it in the church's lobby. Above the cutout, hang a banner that says, "Our preacher is HOTTTTT!!!"

- If you happen to be a physician, write the minister a free, lifetime prescription for Prozac.

- Practice reading your Bible at home, so that when the pastor makes a scriptural reference in her sermon you'll understand what she's talking about and can offer a knowing nod, rather than staring as vacantly as a calf at a new gate.

- During the minister's next sermon, interrupt him every few minutes with thunderous applause and shouts of "Hallelujah! Preach it, brother!"

- Invite him to your house for dinner some night when nobody in the family is (a) dying or (b) furious about the previous week's message.

- Buy her a gift certificate for a weekend at a resort. Little-known tidbit: Preachers like in-room Jacuzzis and hour-long massages as much as normal people do.

- Give him noogies.
- Don't expect the pastor's teenagers to be mini-saints whose primary form of expression is "Praise the Lord." The poor kids are already under enough pressure. Contrary to popular perception, the God gene is only theoretical, not a proven fact.
- Give the minister a big fat salary boost.
- Take him to a UK football game. Manage to endure the entire adventure without asking him to explain Calvin's thoughts on predestination or to justify the deacons' decision to postpone renovating the foyer. Talk about football, and that's it.
- Be gracious to the pastor's husband or wife. The minister's divine calling doesn't guarantee that the spouse can play the organ beautifully or teach the ten-year-olds' Sunday school class.
- Volunteer to serve on a committee—then actually follow through.
- Don't assume that the pastor has memorized the names and playlists of every Christian recording artist in history. He might be an old Molly Hatchet fan.
- Three initials: B.M.W.
- Laugh politely at her cornball jokes. She probably knows some much funnier stories, but can't share those from the pulpit.
- Send him on a sabbatical to the Holy Land. But make sure the plane ticket is round-trip, not stamped "one-way only."
- Try to get along with the other members of the congregation. This will make your minister's life infinitely easier.
- Pray for him, not against him. Pray hard.

PIETY FAILS AS GAUGE
TO EFFECTIVENESS IN OFFICE

October 27, 2007

A h, the election season is full upon us.
Close to home, Republican Gov. Ernie Fletcher and Steve
Beshear, his Democratic challenger, are doing their best to out-Christian each other.

Nationally, the countless presidential hopefuls are leaning on Jesus right and left, so to speak. James Dobson, the evangelical radio personality, has rushed forward to weigh those presidential contenders in the balances—and, like the wall-writing finger of God, mainly has found them wanting.

Praise the Lord and pass the voter registration forms. Here we go again.

All this religious posturing is entertaining. Perhaps it's healthy, a sign of a free and vibrant democracy doing what democracies do best: arguing.

There's nothing new about it. Thomas Jefferson's opponents railed he was unfit to lead the country because he was, they charged, a secret atheist who couldn't keep his pantaloons buttoned. (Am not! Jefferson said.)

Whether he was or wasn't an atheist, whether he did or didn't father children out of wedlock, Jefferson turned out to be a first-rate president. Today his face is on Mount Rushmore.

That's the complicated thing about deciding who to vote for. If you thumb through the history books, you'll find that candidates' religious beliefs and private morality—or for that matter, their party, education, experience or social class—are unreliable predictors of how they'll perform in high office.

According to many historians, our nation's two finest presidents were George Washington and Abraham Lincoln. How different those men were.

Washington was straight out of the 18th century's central casting: regal, socially prominent and a member of his church's vestry (although he didn't take communion and, according to some of his detractors, was known for his profane tongue).

He'd served bravely in a position of terrible responsibility, having led the Continental Army through the dark years of the Revolution. He was held in such esteem that when he made mistakes even his critics tended to blame his underlings; nearly everyone considered Washington himself unassailable.

As for Lincoln, he never joined a church and made few pretensions of religiosity. He was unschooled and hailed from the poorest of families. He was gangly and ugly.

His experience? He'd been elected to a single, two-year term in Congress and defeated in his bids for the Senate.

He had a complicated marriage and a horrible relationship with his father. But Lincoln, too, achieved lasting greatness.

His favorite general, Ulysses Grant, later ran for president. Like Washington, Grant had proved himself a courageous battlefield commander.

Like Lincoln, Grant wasn't pious, but he was honest, humble and loyal. He was a wonderful husband to boot.

Then he became president—and turned out to be among the worst we've had.

Move on to the 20th century.

Scholars rank Franklin Roosevelt's presidency only slightly below, perhaps even equal to, Washington's and Lincoln's. He guided the country through the Depression, then led us to victory in World War II.

A Christian exemplar he wasn't. He was a megalomaniac, and as ruthless as Machiavelli. He routinely deceived friends and foes alike. He was a womanizer.

FDR was followed by Harry Truman. Truman was nominally a Baptist, but not much liked by Baptist leaders. And he mistrusted people he considered too religious.

Politically, he was a product of Kansas City's corrupt Pendergast machine. In the U.S. Senate, he'd compiled an undistinguished record.

We understand now he was a president of incredible foresight who, among other things, probably prevented World War III.

Then there's Jimmy Carter. Conservatives hate Carter's theology, but it's hard to deny that he was among the more devoted Christians ever to occupy the Oval Office, a Sunday school teacher and a man much given to prayer.

Oddly enough, in 1976—the first presidential election in which I was eligible to vote—I cast my ballot for Gerald Ford because I thought Carter was a zealot.

In time, I came to share Carter's faith. Nonetheless, I'd still say he was, to speak charitably of a fellow pilgrim, a mediocre chief executive.

There's just no common pattern here, no reliable way of predicting who will be an able leader and who will be an awful one.

Positions of enormous power—governor, president—carry unique temptations and burdens. Such jobs bring out the best in some people, the worst in others.

In an ideal world, I'd prefer we elect brilliant leaders who also bow to the same God I do. I'd prefer them to be upright in all their ways.

But we don't live in an ideal world. We live in a flawed, fallen world. We're stuck with sinful, complex, self-contradictory humans.

That being so, I'd rather be governed by a competent agnostic than an incompetent believer. I'd rather have Jefferson as president than Carter.

The problem is, none of us can say how well any leader, saint or hedonist, will perform until he or she actually gains the office.

Thus we're destined to follow the campaigns as well as we can, whisper a prayer as we enter the voting booth, push a button—and hold our breath.

THE CONSTANT IN THE PRATHERS' CHRISTMAS

December 22, 2007

My son, John, has announced his engagement to a sweet-natured, pretty young woman named Cassie. This time last year I didn't even know Cassie, and long before next year's Christmas, she'll be my daughter-in-law.

My sister's son, Will, is about to become a father. Will's more like a second son to me than a nephew; he and John practically were raised as brothers. Will's wife, Stephanie, is pregnant with their first child. Next year at the Prathers' annual Christmas gathering, we'll be setting another plate, or at least a jar of baby food.

We've always held our family's celebrations on Christmas Eve, at my parents' house. My mom was one of the best cooks I've ever known, and she spread a holiday feast: country ham with raisin sauce, mashed potatoes, homemade yeast rolls, three or four side dishes, several desserts. I ate until I was contentedly ill.

Mom died in 2003. My dad moved to a smaller house. We still congregate at his place on Christmas Eve, but now we snack on finger foods.

The constituency at those dinners has shifted as well. My sister Cathi's first marriage ended in divorce, but some years later she married Tracy. He brought along T. J., his own son from a previous marriage.

Later still, Cathi and Tracy took in Lorrie, a student from a high school class Cathi taught. They finished raising Lorrie as their daughter. Three years ago, I performed the ceremony in which Lorrie married Ralph, a member of my church. All of them come to the Christmas Eve gathering. Once upon a time we were strangers. We're family now.

139

At my own house, too, the holidays have undergone transformations.

My late wife loved Christmas. Renee sent out scores of cards, shopped months in advance, bought gifts for everyone with whom we were remotely acquainted.

Just after Thanksgiving, she'd put Christmas carols on the stereo, then she and John would spend hours trimming our tree, decorating our house's windows and stringing lights from its gutters. I'd sip custard as I watched the spectacle from the sofa.

After the decorations were finished, Renee would stack and wedge wrapped presents halfway across the den floor.

John and I still share the same home, but we've never been able to work up much enthusiasm about preparing for the holidays.

This year, it was mid-December before we lugged our artificial tree from the basement, hung ornaments on it, and let it go at that. We joked about how bare that corner of the room looked. I hadn't bought, much less wrapped, a single present.

Thinking of his impending marriage, John patted me softly on the shoulder and said, "I guess this is the last time you and I'll be putting up a tree together."

"I suppose that's true," I said.

My girlfriend, Liz, carried over a few colorful packages from her apartment and arranged them under the tree, in part, I think, so it wouldn't appear so forlorn.

Come Christmas Eve, we'll all trek to my father's house with our snacks. There'll be Dad and Cathi and John and Will and me. There'll be Tracy and T. J. and Lorrie and Ralph. There'll be Stephanie and Liz and Cassie.

Christmas, like most things in this world, changes.

That in itself is neither good nor bad. It just is. Some of the changes tear your heart out. Others are joyous—new marriages, new babies, new friendships.

You mourn the old faces that will appear no more. But you also love the new faces you never expected to see. They are bright, wonderful gifts.

And all the while, you try to focus on the only constant, that child born in a Bethlehem stable, who in spirit attended the first Prather Christmas Eve party, and who'll be there again this year, and who has promised to remain with our ever-shifting family through eternity.

I REALLY DON'T KNOW
GOD'S WILL FOR YOU

January 26, 2008

People often come to us ministers for help in making crucial decisions. "Should I marry my fiance despite his obvious flaws?" a woman might ask.

Or, "I think God wants me to quit my career as a banker and go to the seminary. How do I know whether it's really God who's calling me?"

Or, "I've got a job offer in Minneapolis. It pays twice what I'm making now, but maybe I should stay in Lexington to be near my aging parents. What do I choose?"

If Solomon were among us, he could answer such questions. Unfortunately, none of us who works as clergy today is Solomon.

When I'm faced with these types of questions, I never give specific answers.

Generally, I don't know what God wants other folks to do. I have trouble discerning what God wants me to do.

Instead, I suggest a process by which seekers might find their own solutions. It's the same process I use when I'm confused.

If you're among those who believe in God, and you believe he has a benevolent plan for your life, the following exercises might help you see his will more clearly.

Even if you don't believe in any god, or if you believe only in a distant, impersonal deity, several of these suggestions might aid you anyway. They'll help you get in touch with your deepest desires, your truest self.

They are:

- Cut through your own baloney. Do you have a history of falling for every tall, lean, tattooed guy who rides a motorcycle, talks smoothly and treats you badly? Then beware of your infatuation with this suave new six-foot-four biker. He probably isn't The One. Don't rush to the altar with him. It's probably not God telling you to do that. It's probably just you repeating the same old mistakes and telling yourself exactly what you want, but don't need, to hear.

Often God directs us toward people and tasks we normally might not choose.

- Ask whether the option you're considering is moral, legal and compatible with basic scriptural precepts such as, "Do unto others as you'd have them do unto you."

If you're wondering whether God wants you to embark on a career as a loan shark or dump your wife for that titillating little hottie in the next cubicle, the answer is "No."

- Try to surrender your will. Decide you want only to do what's best, whatever that is—and admit you can't possibly know in advance what the best is.

Don't give God instructions: "O Lord, send me to that job in Minneapolis!"

Instead, say to God (or, if you prefer, the great cosmos, or your inner self), "I'll move to Minneapolis or I'll stay in Lexington. I don't care. I just want to know."

Keep repeating that every day until you actually mean it. It's amazing how often you'll quietly discover what you're supposed to do.

- Look for what the Bible calls "the peace that surpasses understanding."

Ignatius of Loyola, a master of spiritual discernment, said that when we're in harmony with God's leadership we tend to feel "consolations" such as courage, deep happiness, gratitude, vitality and freedom. When we're moving away from God, we tend to be discouraged, anxious, burdened, sad and exhausted.

It's a good sign when we find ourselves experiencing unaccountable joy and profound peace even though the external circumstances still look daunting.

• Let God confirm the message. If God is powerful enough to tell you what he wants you to do, he's powerful enough to influence other people as well.

Maybe you suddenly have a burning desire to start a home Bible study group. You suspect this is God speaking to you. If a couple of neighbors then come to you (without any prompting on your part) and say, "You know, we sure wish there was a Bible study group around here," you might safely assume God is confirming what he's already told you.

If you have an overriding urge to move from the research department into marketing, ask God to create an unexpected job opening in marketing and for the marketing director to ask whether you'd be interested in applying for it.

• Wait. For as long as you're still feeling doubt or desperation, do nothing. We get in a hurry; God doesn't. We make bad decisions when we allow ourselves to be motivated by our own impulses, impatience or fear. Until you have an answer that resonates in your soul, stay where you are and keep doing what you're doing.

Granted, these suggestions aren't a sure-fire formula for reading God's mind—or even for reading your own mind. But if you try all these things in conjunction with one another, you're more likely than not to come up with an answer you can live with.

MY SON IS GETTING MARRIED TODAY

February 23, 2008

Today I'll perform the rite in which my only child, John, marries his fiancee, Cassie. Both seem deliriously happy and eager to get on with their future together.

Make the ceremony brief, they've warned me.

That won't be a problem, I've told them.

I intend to employ as few words as is ministerially possible while still leaving them legally wed—because I'm scared I'll break down in the middle of the vows and make a slobbering spectacle of myself.

For this dad, this wedding day is, as Dickens might have put it, the best of times and the worst of times.

I'm so glad for John. I love Cassie, who seems already to have adopted me as a second father. I appreciate the standard cliché—I'm not losing a son but gaining a daughter. That's terrific because I've always wanted a daughter. Now I have one.

And I'm hoping that at some point in the not-too-distant future, I'll also get some grandchildren out of the deal. I can't wait for that.

I realize I'm enormously blessed, compared with the trials other parents have been through. I'll be meeting John today at a church for a wedding, not driving him to rehab or watching him board a troop plane to Iraq or mourning him at a wake.

Still. I'm losing my son. I'm losing my housemate. I'm losing my best friend.

The author of Genesis understood this long ago: "A man shall leave his father and mother," he said, "and cleave to his wife, and they shall become one flesh."

When John says "I do," he quits being primarily my son. He starts being primarily Cassie's husband. That's the way it should be. That's healthy. But I'm having a surprisingly hard time adjusting to this new arrangement. John's been pretty much my constant companion and pretty much my top priority for twenty-four years.

The night he was born, I sat up in a hospital until nearly dawn, waiting on him. His mom had a difficult labor, and we almost lost him. I was there when they pulled him out with forceps. Terrified, I watched the nurse check his vital signs.

Then she wrapped him in a blanket and handed him to me.

"Mr. Prather, meet your son," she said.

At the time he was born, I was in graduate school at the University of Kentucky. I was both studying and teaching classes. When John could walk and talk a bit, I'd take him with me. I'd hold his hand as we crossed the campus.

He wanted to know what everything was: squirrels and leaves and bicycles. When we reached my classroom, I'd give him paper and crayons, sit him in a chair beside my desk, and ask him to be quiet so I could teach. After class, we'd head for Toys R Us.

Later still, I worked for the Herald-Leader. I arrived home one fall afternoon when he was in grade school. As I drove up our cul-de-sac, I saw John in the front yard, wearing his Chicago Bears uniform, pitching a football in the air and running to catch it.

He tripped and fell. He stood up crying.

He'd snapped his collarbone, which was sticking up in an inverted V. His mom and I rushed him to the emergency room. A nurse started to take him away for X-rays.

"I want my dad with me," he said.

And so I went. In the X-ray room, I joked with him about his being the only guy who'd ever suffered a football injury while alone on the field. He managed a smile.

He asked me about the rib I'd broken playing football many years before, and how I'd handled the injury.

"You're a brave boy," I said. "You can do this."

And we did.

When John was a teenager, his mom was diagnosed with cancer. After she passed away, he stayed here with me. I told people we'd become less father and son than two bachelors sharing the same digs.

Countless nights, he and I watched old black-and-white movies and talked past midnight. On the weekends, I'd go see his rock band perform.

We took vacations to places like New Orleans, New York, San Francisco and Palm Springs. In a Louisiana swamp, he jumped out of our tour boat onto a mossy bank to pet a wild, ten-foot alligator our guide had spotted.

Today, everything will change. We'll finish the wedding ceremony, then John and Cassie will start off on their honeymoon, start off on their new life.

I'll come back to a house that suddenly seems ungodly big and silent.

THE OLDER I GET, THE LESS I JUDGE

April 26, 2008

L ast month I turned fifty-two. It was something of a shock. Fifty-two isn't decrepit, but it's sure a lot older than I used to be.

I still think of myself as being about twenty-six—until I pass by a mirror or a plate-glass window and see my late grandfather, Fred Prather, staring back at me.

As you age, a lot of things change besides your looks.

I've written this before, but one thing I find different in my own life is that, the older I get, the less I judge people.

Basically, I don't judge anybody anymore for anything.

I mentioned this in a speech I gave recently. In the question-and-answer session that followed my talk, a member of the audience asked me to explain what I meant.

For instance, does that mean I find all behaviors equal? Does it mean I'm against, let's say, convicting felons of their crimes and sending them to jail?

No, I don't mean that. Not at all.

In my opinion, we probably do send way too many people to jail. But to borrow a line from Richard Pryor, I still say, "Thank God we have prisons."

If I were to sit on a jury, I'd vote to send certain criminals away. There are careers thugs who prey on the innocent, who maim, rob and pillage time and again.

They're called Congress. (Ha! That's a joke!)

Seriously, there are some people who are dangerous, who definitely ought to be locked up where they can't hurt their fellow humans.

But what I'm trying to say is this: the older I get, the less willing I am to judge other people's hearts or relationships with the Almighty.

I don't know who's truly evil and who's good, who's going to heaven and who's going to hell. Those are God's calls, not mine, and I find myself increasingly happy to leave the verdicts up to him.

Even in the case of a career criminal, I can never know all the factors that made him the person he is. I can't know his secret thoughts.

He may have been malnourished, abandoned or tortured as a toddler. He may have suffered a brain injury in a car wreck that affected his ability to control his impulses. He may hate the things he does and pray every night for forgiveness and to be delivered from the demons that drive him.

The point is, I don't know.

So it's not my place to condemn him as a human being. It's not my place to decide whether he's one of God's children. It's not my place to look down on him.

It is my place to remember: there but by the grace of God go I. Every day, it's my place to extend that grace and the benefit-of-the-doubt to malefactors great and small.

I knew a young woman who was married and a mother. She was attractive, funny, college-educated and held a professional job. She seemed to have everything.

When a mutual friend told me she was also conducting a long-term affair with a much older man, I was surprised—and, frankly, put off.

Time went on. I got to know her better. I learned that as a kid she'd been raped by the father of a playmate. Her own family had endured a murder and a suicide.

Her husband was a closet addict who spent much of his time unemployed. Her only child suffered from an incurable, debilitating disease; she was the primary caregiver.

The more I learned, the more I understood why she might have made some of the choices she made. After a while, she became one of my heroes. I couldn't imagine how she functioned as well as she did.

149

I was pretty sure that if I'd had to deal with all she'd dealt with, I would have done a lot of worse things than she'd done.

I'm not trying to justify her affair. It's not my job to justify it.

But it's not my job to condemn her, either.

I'm simply saying that, when we look at people superficially, going by outward appearances, focusing on their mistakes, it's easy to wag our heads self-righteously.

But there's no way of calculating how many things we don't know about them. You and I have no idea what they're struggling with, what they've been through.

And since we don't know, we're in no position to judge.

In God's sight, they might be far better people than we are.

THE BEST BIRTHDAY PRESENT EVER

May 24, 2008

In late March we had a small party for my fifty-second birthday. My girlfriend, Liz, cooked dinner for me and my son, John, my daughter-in-law, Cassie, and my dad.

After the meal, I opened a birthday card from John and Cassie. Its cover read, "Wise. Generous. Helpful. Occasionally goofy. Quick with a hug. Full of great advice. It's a grandpa thing."

The message didn't register.

Inside, the card's print said: "Thanks for doing it so well. Happy birthday, Grandpa!" I still didn't get it.

Then I saw that John had scrawled in his own hand: "Best birthday present ever? We love you! Love, John and Cassie."

Best birthday present ever?

I looked across the table at John.

He nodded. Cassie smiled.

I lost my mind. I screamed, threw the card straight up in the air, leapt from my chair and ran around the table, arms outspread. Or so they told me later.

Liz was already running around the table from the other side, shrieking and hugging them.

Yep. I'm going to be a grandfather.

I probably shouldn't call it a full-on miracle, but it's certainly a surprise.

Before their February wedding, John and Cassie had warned me this day might never come. Like many otherwise healthy women, Cassie is plagued with endometriosis, and her gynecologist said that could make it difficult for her to get pregnant.

151

If she hoped to ever have a child, the doctor said, she should start trying as soon as possible after the wedding, and after the honeymoon she should start taking fertility drugs. Even so, it probably would take quite a while for her to conceive.

So John and Cassie went on their honeymoon to Jamaica without bothering with birth control, without thinking it was even an issue. Cassie got pregnant that first week.

She was shocked. John was shocked. The doctor was shocked.

I was shocked, too—and tee-totally thrilled.

I haven't been the same since they told me.

I find myself walking around town with a stupid grin spread over my face. When prospective tenants come to inspect one of the apartments I own—strangers, mind you—I find myself blurting out, apropos of nothing, "I'm going to be a grandfather."

In the grocery the other day, I bumped into our local high school principal, who was with his two grandchildren.

"I'm about to become a grandpa myself," I announced.

"There's nothing like it," he said. "It'll make you goofy."

Goofy isn't even the word. John brings by the latest grainy ultrasound photos. I sit on the couch and study them like they're vital documents of state.

I can't decide what to do first, open a college fund or buy a swing set.

John and Cassie are concerned about childcare, since they both work full-time.

"I'll help keep the baby," I've said. "If I have to go to a church meeting or tend my apartments, I can take the kid with me. But let me forewarn you—whenever I'm in babysitting, there will be no discipline. This child can't possibly do anything wrong that I would ever need to correct. As far as I'm concerned, everything this baby does is wonderful."

And the poor kid's not even here yet. Lord only knows what an idiot I'll be once I can actually hold it in my arms.

I've been thinking quite a bit about my maternal grandfather, Oscar Chestnut. He was one of the more influential people in my life. I loved him completely.

A farmer, he'd broken down his health toiling his difficult piece of land. My grandmother used to fret over him.

I remember once overhearing her tell my mom, "But you know what? Oscar can be dragging around, barely moving, one foot already in the grave. Then Paul David shows up, and he's a different man. He's out in the yard playing tag and laughing and cackling like a kid himself. It's hard to believe."

I remember how Papa's face used to light up every time he'd see me getting out of the car, heading toward him. God love him.

Today, I haven't even met my grandchild yet, and I'm already lit up.

WHY EVANGELICALS' INFLUENCE
IS DECLINING

June 28, 2008

arlier this month, the *Herald-Leader* carried an op-ed piece that
detailed a dramatic erosion in the numbers and social influence of
U.S. evangelical Christians.

The author was Christine Wicker, a former religion reporter for *The
Dallas Morning News*, who has a new book, *The Fall of the Evangelical Nation: The Surprising Crisis Inside the Church.*

Wicker pointed out, for example, that the largest evangelical denomination, the Southern Baptist Convention, is declining so steadily
that, if current trends continue, half its 43,000 churches will be forced
to close by 2030.

I agree that evangelical Christianity is losing ground. Wicker offered three explanations, while acknowledging that other factors also
have contributed to the trend.

I'd argue for a fourth major reason, one Wicker mentioned but
dismissed.

Here are Wicker's explanations.

First, the rise of Alcoholics Anonymous and other twelve-step pro-
grams created a type of contemporary American faith based loosely on
Christianity, but without the evangelical demands for a salvation
experience, personal guilt or adherence to doctrines.

"Nothing like that kind of open-ended faith had ever been experienced before," Wicker wrote.

Americans are moving toward similar faith systems that offer them
more freedom.

Second, the ease with which we now travel and communicate
across cultures has transformed evangelicals themselves. When people

154

live in small, insular communities, it's convenient for them to believe they possess God's only word to humanity, that they alone know the path to salvation and should share it with their neighbors.

As international travel and immigration have become commonplace, as we've become accustomed to seeing other cultures daily on TV and the internet, it's become difficult for any group to claim they're the only ones saved.

All those "other people" evangelicals once thought were cut off from God, today are "likely to be your son-in-law or grandchild," Wicker said.

So evangelicals feel less zealous.

Third, the Pill started a moral shift for which evangelicals were totally unprepared. Given the ability to have sex without fear of pregnancy, huge numbers of people postponed marriage and started living together outside wedlock.

Evangelical churches either shrilly condemned this or else, at the other end of the spectrum, ignored it.

"But evangelicals' failure to grapple with change," Wicker said, "meant the church was no help in a world where people were expected to sleep together long before marriage and desperately sought guidance about when and with whom."

Wicker's theories are thought-provoking. Each contains an element of truth.

However, I think there's another reason evangelicals find their influence waning. I'd say it might be the primary cause.

Too often, evangelicals have taken their greatest gift—the most liberating and exciting message in the world's history—and pounded it into a heap of unsightly rubble.

The core of the evangelical message is, or should be, that we've all been offered by God an unfathomable mercy, an undeserved grace, an unconditional acceptance.

The person they—or, we (for I am an evangelical)—claim to be our founder, said he came to proclaim the favorable year of the Lord, to assure us God is no longer holding our sins against us, to let us know God profoundly loves this world and everyone in it.

When he met a Samaritan woman who'd been married multiple times and was living with a guy she wasn't married to, he didn't point his finger at her. Instead, he turned her into a messenger of grace who touched off a local revival.

When he ran into a dishonest, conniving tax collector, Jesus invited himself to the man's house for supper. The man was so flabbergasted by this gesture of acceptance that he reformed his ways.

And yet the folks we evangelicals have appointed as our public mouthpieces usually seem to be people who wouldn't recognize Jesus if he walked down the center aisle of their church wearing a red derby hat.

They define themselves, and us, by what they're against, and they're against just about everything and everybody: abortion, gay marriage, Jews, Catholics, Muslims, Hollywood, liberals, feminists. They're even against other, competing evangelicals.

Oddly, they apparently aren't against the government's attempts to legalize torture. I've yet to hear a sermon against that.

I remember that one Christian writer (I think it was Philip Yancey, but can't locate the passage) said he conducted his own informal survey of non-churchgoers. He asked them what came to their minds when they heard the term "evangelical Christian."

They invariably described evangelicals as hypocritical, mean and self-righteous.

Not one person, he said, thought evangelicals were kind or forgiving or helpful.

In her op-ed piece, Wicker mentioned this image problem as a reason some evangelicals give for their movement's decline. But she discounts it.

I don't discount it.

I can't say that if evangelical leaders suddenly stepped off their soap boxes and started washing strangers' dusty feet, the movement would explode with new members. But, at the very least, we'd be imparting to the world a more accurate image of the master we claim to serve.

MORE THOUGHTS
ON THE EVANGELICAL DECLINE

July 12, 2008

My last column horrified some folks.

I wrote that too often we evangelical Christians have taken our greatest gift—the most liberating, exciting message in history—and pounded it into rubble.

The core of the evangelical message should be that God offers all humans an unfathomable mercy, an undeserved acceptance. But typically we've appointed as our mouth-pieces people who define themselves, and us, by what they're against, and they're against just about everything and everybody. They're even against other evangelicals.

My observations lighted fires under several readers, one or two of whom warned that I'm preaching "cheap grace." This is evangelical code, a term that, leveled against another Christian, constitutes the ultimate insult.

It means you're wishy-washy on sin, that you're saying Christians can misuse God's love as a convenient excuse to avoid having any moral standards.

I'm grateful to my critics. No, really, I am. They help me understand how others perceive my comments.

So let me elaborate. First, I've never argued that grace is cheap. If the evangelical message is true, no one could call grace cheap. According to our theology, grace cost God his only son. It cost Jesus his position in heaven (he became one of us, which was a sacrifice we can't fathom). It cost him his life.

St. John quotes Jesus as saying the reason he and his heavenly father were willing to pay such prices is that they loved the world. God didn't send Jesus to judge the world, Jesus said, but to rescue us, its inhabitants, from ourselves.

To my mind, if the Lord continues to love "the world," that means he loves men and women, blacks and whites, Jews and Christians, Muslims and pagans.

Second, I've never said anyone's sins are OK. My view of human nature cannot be described as, "I'm OK, you're OK." My view is, "I'm a train wreck, and you're probably worse." Actions, good or bad, have consequences. You and I alike have committed our share of stupid, evil deeds. We've hurt ourselves and those around us.

The big question for evangelicals, though, is where we put our emphasis when we're reaching out to our suffering fellow humans. I believe our duty is to exhibit a lot of mercy and joy, and hardly any recrimination and condemnation.

We rarely need to point out other people's sins. Most reprobates I've met already know they're messed up. Besides, they know we're sinners, too. Even if we succeed in making them feel guilty, they'll resent being led to the gallows by hypocrites.

I've been an evangelical almost all my life. If I've learned anything, it's that evangelicals are as screwy as any other group of people.

Sad to say, even after they become Christians, evangelicals feud, fornicate, divorce, get abortions, take dope, cheat at business and create dysfunctional families at about the same rates as non-believers.

I'm not arguing that's how it ought to be. That's the way it is.

You have no idea the secrets the person sitting next to you in the pew, or standing in a pulpit, carries. If you knew, you'd freak out. Or cry. Or run away.

Even worse, evangelicals feel pressured into being hypocritical about such matters. We feel compelled to maintain a religious facade. Often we're terrified of honesty—for fear our fellow evangelicals will shun us. We lie to our parents, to our ministers, to our fellow churchgoers, to our spouses, to our children.

But what should set Christians apart is, despite our myriad failures, we have hope. That's the wonder of the Christian message: There is forgiveness. There is redemption. Every day's a new start.

Our primary message should be that God loves everybody—gays, women who've had abortions, NRA members, neo-Nazis, Rhodes Scholars, felons, addicts, Jews, feminists, journalists, Hollywood actors, the Taliban.

You name them, God loves them.

St. Paul says God loves even those who blatantly hate him.

Sure, God doesn't always agree with what we do, before or after we become Christians. And disagreement does sometimes entail correction. But with God, correction doesn't come first. Love comes first. He's willing to accept us just as we are.

It's a profound principle, yet not a complicated one.

Acceptance isn't the same as agreement. The beauty of God is that he can disagree with our choices, with our actions, with our thoughts, and go right on loving us.

That's how we Christians are supposed to love others. We're to focus on their intrinsic worth, not on their faults. We're to graciously accept them, not chase them off.

Because we're as flawed as anyone. That's a powerful thing to remember.

We all stand in need of God's grace, every last one of us.

A RETURN TO JOY

July 26, 2008

It's a girl!

I'm officially nuts now. I'm truly unhinged.

Last week, I drove my pregnant daughter-in-law, Cassie, and my girlfriend, Liz, to meet my son at the office of Cassie's ob-gyn in Winchester.

It was the big event, the day we would discover whether Cassie is carrying a boy or a girl. I was honored that she and John asked me along.

They issued the invitation spontaneously, out of the goodness of their hearts. I only had to beg three or four times, "Can I go? Please? Please?"

They invited Liz, too, I'm pretty sure in the hope she'd stop me from embarrassing myself—and them.

The doctor's office apparently has a rule that only two people can accompany the expectant mother into the room where the ultrasound is performed. Liz waited in the lobby, while John and I went in with Cassie.

Cassie stretched out on an examining table. The technician flipped off the lights. She touched the wand to Cassie's belly. We watched a TV screen mounted on the wall.

And there that little sweetie was, right before my eyes, all one pound of her.

Oh, she put on a show. She played with her hands. She kicked her legs. She did a somersault, trying to escape the annoyance of the buzzing wand.

We saw her eyes, nose and mouth. We saw her spine, liver and pumping heart.

And we saw that she's a she.

I tried to act mature. As we watched the TV, I limited myself to profound statements such as, "Mmm" and "Is that her spine or the umbilical cord?"

"Are you OK?" John asked me.

"Sure," I said. "Why wouldn't I be?"

"You're awfully quiet," he said.

I think he expected me to drop to my knees, slap the tiles with my palms and shriek like a hyena. He's spent twenty-five years with me, after all.

Afterward, we returned to the waiting room and told Liz what we'd learned. We showed her still photos taken from the ultrasound video. She giggled.

The four of us went outside and stood on the sidewalk chatting.

"Are you OK?" John asked me.

"I'm fine."

At last, Cassie and John got in John's car.

Liz and I climbed into my car. I waved goodbye to John and Cassie.

As they pulled away, I fell over on Liz's shoulder and wept.

I hope not to wax melodramatic, but I never thought I'd survive to see this day.

Just a few years ago, I was at the lowest point of my life, convulsed by family tragedies. I developed diabetes, hypertension, depression. I wasted away spiritually, physically and emotionally.

I became convinced I'd collapse any day of a heart attack or stroke. I'd be gone long before John could marry and have kids.

Yet here I am.

Of course, along with my immeasurable joy, I also feel sorrow. I wish my wife, Renee, had lived to see our grandbaby. I wish my mom could see her. They'd be ecstatic.

I don't have a clue why God allowed Renee and my mom to die and let me live. Both of them were better people than I am. I have a lot of questions to ask the Lord if and when I make it to heaven. For now, the situation just is what it is.

There was a time, when I was younger, that I counted myself the most blessed man in Kentucky. I had a lovely and devoted wife, a terrific son, perfect health, jobs I loved, plenty of money. I thought all that would last forever.

It didn't. Through no real fault of our own, my family and I fell into a hell we couldn't foresee—disease, darkness, turmoil. I began to think that would last forever.

It didn't. Therein is both our curse as humans and our blessing: whatever we're experiencing, it will pass.

Today, once more, I'm overwhelmed with joy and gratitude. When I do leave this world, I'll leave knowing I've seen my beautiful grand-daughter.

Today, I'm again the happiest man in the Commonwealth. And the cause for much of my delight is kicking and rolling and blinking in Cassie's womb.

TORTURE IS NEITHER CHRISTIAN
NOR AMERICAN

August 9, 2008

The most disturbing revelation about our government in quite a while is the ongoing disclosure that, after 9/11, the Bush administration embraced what Vice President Cheney euphemistically called "the dark side."

That is, the administration secretly adopted an official program of torture against suspected enemy combatants captured in Iraq, Afghanistan and elsewhere.

Abu Ghraib was not an exception, not the result of a few sadistic enlisted soldiers run amok. We now know Abu Ghraib was just one manifestation of a policy in which the abuse of prisoners was ordered, and at times micro-managed, from the highest offices in Washington, D.C.

The approved tactics included not only waterboarding prisoners, which has gotten a lot of publicity, but sexually humiliating them, depriving them of sleep, terrorizing them with dogs and shackling them in excruciating positions.

This should appall every American.

What perplexes me most, though, is that the great majority of U.S. Christians seem to be reacting to this sordid news with a long, corporate yawn.

It's been only ten years since many of these same Christians—from TV evangelists to radio pundits to local pastors to folks in the pew—were calling for Bill Clinton's impeachment. Hey, they were screaming for his head on a pike.

His offense? He'd dallied with a willing intern in the Oval Office.

"How dare he?" Christians cried. "Reprobate! Sinner!"

Now we learn the current administration committed—not a few times, but concertedly, for years—crimes both evil and medieval. And Christians don't care.

I'm still trying to figure that one out.

One reason for Christians' collective silence may be that Bush, Cheney and their advisers are conservative Republicans, as are a great many Christians, especially the white evangelicals who despised Clinton so vocally and voted for Bush so heavily.

But torture isn't an issue that should pit Democrats against Republicans, or liberals against conservatives. It's a foundational moral issue. It should pit all decent people against barbarians. It's not about right and left. It's about right and wrong.

Indeed, many of the folks most horrified by the administration's policy have been the ones assigned to help implement it, from senior military officers (clearly not a bunch of bleeding hearts) to mid-level members of the administration itself (presumably all staunch conservatives).

Whether individual critics line up to the right or left, their reasoning has been identical: Torture is despicable by any measure—it's uncivilized, it's un-American and, in a practical sense, it's tragically counterproductive.

It produces worthless military intelligence, since agonized prisoners will tell interrogators anything they want to hear, true or not. Torture also diminishes America's standing among our allies and provides our enemies with an incomparable recruiting tool.

Worst of all, torture destroys the American ethos. We like to view our country as a beacon of enlightenment and freedom. Torturing people makes us feel like fascists.

So where's the hue and cry against Bush, Cheney, John Yoo, the former Justice Department lawyer said to have developed the arguments "legalizing" torture, and David Addington, the vice president's enforcer on this issue? The only message I can infer from Christians' silence is this: To them, what Clinton did with Monica Lewinsky was more reprehensible than what American interrogators and their surrogates in Egypt did to Mamdouh Habib, an Australian captured in Pakistan, who was tormented with electric cattle prods and threatened with rape by dogs. As Dahlia Lithwick wrote in Newsweek, Habib "confessed to all sorts of things that weren't true" until, after three years, he was released—without charges.

Why is it Christians, followers of the Prince of Peace, followers of the one who commanded us to love our enemies, don't find these offenses worthy of impeachment?

Perhaps, in many American Christians' minds, the people we've captured in Iraq, Afghanistan or Pakistan represent Satan—they're Taliban, they're Al Qaeda. They're killers who crash airliners into skyscrapers and saw the heads off their prisoners. They look different than we do. They follow a different religion.

But it's important to remember that investigator after investigator has found that the majority of people we've imprisoned and brutalized aren't Al Qaeda or Taliban. Many are innocent farmers or merchants snatched up mistakenly in the chaos of war.

Besides, the bottom line is, we Americans are supposed to be better than the Taliban. The Taliban live in the 7th century; we live in the 21st. We're the good guys.

The United States has in the past faced ruthless enemies and perilous threats to our existence. During such times, previous administrations have ignored certain human rights, too. But no administration has ever sunk so low as to actively promote torture.

So where is Christians' outrage?

If torturing your enemies isn't a sin, there's no such thing as a sin.

EVANGELICAL, PENTECOSTAL,
AND REASONABLE

September 27, 2008

When describing my religious beliefs, I usually call myself an evangelical and a Pentecostal. But these terms, at least when appropriated by yours truly, tend to provoke consternation.

My fellow evangelicals and Pentecostals, having read my columns, often assume I'm a heretic. Those willing to admit I could, in theory, be one of Jesus' sheep, think I'm a black sheep. They hesitate to claim me.

And people of other or no religious leanings shake their heads, too.

"But you're so ... so ... reasonable," they say. "You can't be one of "—envision a pinching of the nostrils— "'those' people."

Well, yes, friends, I am. Lock, stock and Billy Graham Fan Club button.

The confusion stems from a widespread misunderstanding of what "evangelical" and "Pentecostal" mean. Today, even evangelicals and Pentecostals themselves seem not to know the histories of their movements.

I spent my first twenty-one years among the Southern Baptists, a baptized member, from age six, of the largest evangelical denomination. Almost from my arrival in the delivery room, I was indoctrinated with Baptist lore.

I received generous doses of Roger Williams, the founder of the Baptist faith in America. Williams, zealous about his own beliefs, couldn't figure why every straight-thinking person didn't see it his way. (Sounds like my Baptist grandmother.)

Yet he helped forge Rhode Island into the most tolerant colony on the continent, an oasis in a land of religious persecution. He shielded Jews, Quakers and Indians alike.

He preached "soul liberty," the idea that every human has a right to seek God, or not, exactly as he or she sees fit, without interference.

He distrusted governmental involvement in religion and religion's involvement in government. It was Williams who, in 1644, coined the term "wall of separation" to describe his belief that state and church ought to studiously avoid each other.

Eventually, I left the Baptists, but I remained an evangelical.

By definition, an evangelical places the Bible's authority above creeds or sacraments, believes in the salutary effects of a personal conversion and thinks it's helpful to share the good news of Jesus' mercy and grace with anyone who asks (or who is at least willing to listen to the speaker blather on).

Check. Check. Check.

The term evangelical shouldn't be used as a synonym for "right-wing crank." Many evangelicals today are conservative Republicans, which is fine. That's not a synonym for right-wing crank, either.

But earlier evangelicals were extraordinarily liberal.

In his 1990 book *Under God: Religion and American Politics*, historian Garry Wills reminds us that William Jennings Bryan, the foremost evangelical of the late 1800s and early 1900s, was also the most progressive statesman of his era.

An ailing, aged, addled Bryan was nationally humiliated during the 1925 Scopes Monkey Trial. He died days afterward of diabetes.

But in his prime he'd been a three-time Democratic nominee for president and Woodrow Wilson's secretary of state. As Wills notes, "His campaigns were the most leftist mounted by a major party candidate in our entire history."

Among other things, Bryan fought for women's suffrage, strict regulation of big business and the abolition of capital punishment.

He apparently developed his views from having read—and believed—the New Testament, which tells us that men and women are equal in God's eyes, that God favors the poor over the rich and that God's children should treat prisoners compassionately.

Historically, then, the term evangelical has included myriad interpretations of the Gospel and its commandments.

Finally, I'm a Pentecostal. Scholars generally trace Pentecostalism to the Azusa Street revival that erupted in 1906 in Los Angeles.

In a time of brutal segregation, the three-year revival, led by a black preacher, W. J. Seymour, was amazing for its egalitarianism. White Southerners traveled to sit at Seymour's feet. Women took the pulpit. People of all stations worshiped side-by-side.

Those early Pentecostals also believed God was restoring the gifts of the Holy Spirit recorded in the Acts of the Apostles, such as prophecy, healing and tongues.

I love the idea that God might break into any given church meeting and replace our agenda with something better.

I love the fervor of Pentecostal worship. I'm by nature emotionally constrained. It's therapeutic for me to feel free to raise my hands in praise or even to cry. I've had a lot, good and bad, to cry about. It's healthy to let it out.

Plus, Pentecostal music rocks.

My point is, we evangelicals and Pentecostals can be liberals, centrists or conservatives, all the while obeying God to the best of our abilities.

We're allowed to interpret the scriptures by our own lights, even as our neighbors draw different meanings from the same passages.

We can share our faith with those who want to hear it, without feeling compelled to bludgeon into submission those who don't.

It's entirely possible to be an evangelical and a Pentecostal and yet be kind, tolerant and reasonable.

I'M A GRANDFATHER

November 8, 2008

Harper Renee Prather was born at 8:10 p.m. on Monday in Winchester.

No offense to anyone else's child or grandchild, but I'm compelled by journalistic integrity to tell the truth: She's far and away the most beautiful baby in Kentucky.

Or in the U.S.A. Or in the cosmos.

She's got a head full of dark hair. She's got rosebud lips. She weighs seven pounds, two ounces, and is nineteen inches long.

She hasn't said much yet, but it's clear she's the smartest kid around, too. You ought to see how brilliantly she wiggles her long thin toes. Genius. Pure genius.

I'm a grandfather.

My son John and daughter-in-law Cassie named the baby after Harper Lee, the author of *To Kill a Mockingbird*, and after John's mom, my late wife Renee.

The baby's even got a perfect name.

Harper wasn't due until November 19. Cassie's nurse-midwife decided to induce labor early because Cassie's blood pressure kept rising and her legs were swelling badly.

We all trekked to the hospital Sunday night—John, Cassie, Cassie's family, my girlfriend Liz and I.

Cassie's dad, Bobby Hudson, breeds Tennessee walking horses. He's spent many long nights waiting for mares to foal.

After the nurses had put Cassie in her bed and started an IV, Bobby said, "Reckon I should go on and get a fresh bale of hay and put it in here?"

169

It became clear nothing was going to happen Sunday night.

I eventually went home. The next morning, after I'd returned, John told me he and Cassie had only slept about an hour.

We waited all day Monday. At one point, John and I took a short drive down the road to find a box of "It's a girl!" cigars for him to hand out.

Later, I left the hospital to get myself some lunch. While I was out, I picked up an order of fast-food fish for John.

Cassie was dozing in the labor room. The nurses already had assigned her a second room where she'd be moved after the baby arrived. It was empty.

John and I slipped into that more private room so he could eat. He sat in a rocking chair, munching fish and french fries. He'd barely finished when I heard him snoring.

As I looked at him, sitting there exhausted in that rocker, his legs crossed at the ankles, I thought of the night twenty-five years ago when his mother and I waited until 4:40 a.m. for him to arrive.

I thought of the soccer games and school plays and graduations Renee and I had attended. I thought about how proud Renee would be of him today.

I thought of the years John and I nursed his mom through cancer, and the years he and I shared a house after her death. I thought of vacations he and I had taken to New Orleans and San Francisco and Los Angeles.

I thought about where our journey together might take us still.

When Harper finally did decide to come, she did it quickly. By then, perhaps two dozen family and friends were gathered in the hallway outside the labor room.

John, Cassie's mom, Debbie, and Bobby rushed inside to help with the delivery. Someone shut the door. A security guard stalked down the hall and shooed everyone back to the empty room where Cassie would be moved later.

Cassie's grandmother, Evelyn, and I declined to leave, security guard or not.

170

We pressed our ears against the metal door.

By and by, we heard the squalling of a baby.

Evelyn burst into tears and hugged me.

I wheeled and pressed my way into the labor room before the attendants had finished cleaning Cassie or the baby. Nurses wiped Harper's chest and arms beneath a heat lamp. I snapped pictures of her, my heart thumping. Oh, I thought, she has no idea how many people love her already.

John walked over and stood beside me. Tears trickled down his cheeks.

Sometime afterward—details of time and sequence became blurry—Cassie had been washed and covered up.

I made my way to her bedside. I bent and kissed her on the forehead.

"Thank you," I said.

She smiled. "You're welcome." She looked tired and satisfied.

A nurse carried Harper, wrapped now in a blanket, back to Cassie. Cassie lifted the baby to John for the first time.

"Hi," he whispered, gazing at Harper's tiny, clenched eyes. "I'm your dad."

I was looking over his shoulder. But I kept my silence. I didn't want to intrude on that moment.

What I wanted to say was, "Son, you are so blessed to have her. But she's equally blessed to have you. And I am inexpressibly grateful to have you both."

MEMORY OF FIRELIGHT

November 22, 2008

Becoming a grandfather has got me reminiscing again about my own grandfathers, Oscar Chestnut and Fred Prather, both of whom lived in Pulaski County, both of whom have been dead a long time.

Papa Chestnut, for instance, was a farmer in the Oak Hill community. When I was a small boy, the clapboard house he and my grandmother lived in still didn't have an indoor bathroom or central heat.

One winter, my parents and I traveled to the farm in the midst of a blizzard. It must have been around Christmas, because otherwise we wouldn't have been making the journey from Berea, where we lived then, through weather like that.

I was four or five years old.

My dad had put chains on our car's tires, but we got bogged down anyway in the rough, narrow lane that led to Papa's house. We were stuck for quite a while.

I pulled off a mitten, so I could grip my cap pistol. Against my mother's protests, I clambered out of the car to tromp around in snow that reached to my knees.

Papa and my dad tried to rock the car loose. They dug around the wheels with shovels. As they labored, they expelled puffs of steam from their mouths. Snowflakes stuck to their caps and coats. They debated whether to tow the car out with Papa's tractor.

"I'll shoot the snow off the tires," I said, waving my six-gun.

Papa leaned on his shovel. "Give her a try, cowpoke. It sure beats this digging."

That night, my mother tucked me into a feather bed. The pillowcase and sheets were cold, but the down mattress enveloped me. Mom covered me with several homemade quilts. The whole bed smelled of must. My parents climbed into another bed in the same room. In minutes, I was snug and sound asleep.

I was awakened in the dark by a shuffling sound, someone moving. I raised my head and felt the room's frigid air nip my ears.

I saw Papa, in silhouette, on one knee before the fireplace, which had nearly burned out. He dropped chunks of coal on the grate, then jabbed the coal with a poker. Sparks raced up the chimney. He added more coal. In moments, the fire roared red and yellow. Strange shadows danced off the walls.

Before my eyes closed again, the last thing I saw was him still crouched by the fireplace, guarding the blaze.

The next morning, my parents, my grandparents and I sat down at a claw-foot table to the huge farmer's breakfast my grandmother fixed every day: eggs and sausage and biscuits and gravy and coffee and tall glasses of milk from Papa's cows. The milk had bits of cream floating on it. A coal-burning stove warmed the kitchen.

"Papa, I saw you in our room last night," I said.

"He was building the fire," my mom said.

"I know. Why did you do that?"

Papa ladled gravy onto his biscuits. "I got to thinking that you're a town boy, and you're used to a house with a good furnace. I was afraid you'd get cold. Maybe get sick."

He said this casually, off-handedly. We went on with our breakfast.

As far as I can recall, nobody ever mentioned this tiny incident again.

It puzzled me, though. I knew how cold it was in that old house in the middle of the night. I knew I'd been toasty in my feather bed and that, across the room, my parents had been equally cozy in theirs. They hadn't gotten up to stoke the fire.

But Papa had. He'd interrupted his sleep, left his own warm bed and felt his way down a frigid, black hall. For me.

That image of him kneeling by the fireplace remains with me nearly a half-century later.

Now that I'm a grandfather myself, I finally understand why he was there.

EPILOGUE

December, 2008

As I write these closing words in December 2008, three-and-a-half years have elapsed since Renee's death. I thought I might never be able to say this, but I've begun to bear more resemblance to my old self—the guy whose mind and bones I inhabited before Renee was stricken with cancer—than to the frail, wounded, exhausted, scared man who struggled alongside her through her illness and death.

I'm healing. I rarely break into tears for no discernable reason. I still endure stabs of loneliness or regret, but they're briefer and less disabling than before.

I've dated one woman, Liz, for a long time. Initially, going out with her felt as if I were betraying Renee, even though Renee was gone. Sometimes I felt as if my romantic emotions, my ability to experience infatuation, had been buried with my wife. But that's changed, too. My emotions weren't really dead, only hibernating. They've emerged from their cave.

The birth of my granddaughter, Harper Renee, was a godsend. She's only a few weeks old, but already I've experienced a depth of joy I didn't think I was capable of anymore. To my surprise and gratitude, I find that I am capable.

And I again feel stirrings of my old faith in a God whose chief traits are, I think, love and grace, rather than a stony silence broken only by occasional acts of cruelty. I find myself going to church eagerly rather than out of professional compulsion.

I have hope: For Liz, for my church, for John and Cassie, for Harper, for myself.

The flesh sometimes is capable of recovering, I suppose, and so is the spirit.

174

I'm not the man I was before Renee got sick. My friends and family, who don't agree on much, agree on that. Some think I'm actually a better person than I was eight years ago; others think the opposite.

Those who view the changes in me as not particularly salutary say that, for instance, I'm less animated in my preaching, less certain of myself and my doctrines.

Others look at those shifts and tell me I'm less cocky, more mature, more compassionate, more apt to pose questions than to assume I hold the answers.

As I ruminate on those years of caregiving and on the time I've spent as a survivor, I remain confounded by the whole ordeal.

I don't know why Renee, young and in no recognized risk group, contracted cancer. I regret my failings as a caregiver, wish I'd been stronger, less angry, more tender. I'd give anything for another chance to sit with Renee during her illness, to do a better job. But that's impossible. The past is what it is. No one can change it.

Oddly, I find comfort in the past, too. Before Renee fell ill, we had more than twenty years of wonderful marriage, and I remember all those great years. After she was diagnosed with cancer, and, as our lives descended into a pit that seemed to have no floor, I stayed with her. I remained faithful to her, to our son, to our church.

I take comfort from Romans 8, in which Paul assures us that God causes all things to work together for good to those who love him. The strength Renee exhibited during her battle touched everyone with whom she dealt. Who can say what fruit her struggle will bear, even though she's not here? And my own experiences have encouraged thousands of other caregivers and survivors, through my *Herald-Leader* columns, through speeches I've given around Kentucky, and now, I trust, through this book.

I've considered St. Paul's life—although I'm in no way likening my spiritual influence to his. St. Paul spent a chunk of his ministry locked away in dirty, dreadful jails. He was an apostle, but he also was a human being. Those incarcerations must have been agonizing for him, as they would be for any person. He must have wondered why

175

God would allow him to be shut off from the churches he cared about so deeply, why he was allowed to sit alone, lonesome and idle.

But from his jail cells—because he couldn't reach his mission churches in person—he wrote letters that explained his beliefs, described his sufferings and exhorted his fellow Christians to keep the faith. Those letters now comprise much of the New Testament and have changed the course of humanity. They've touched infinitely more people than Paul could have spoken to in person had he been a free man. He might never have written his epistles had he not been sent to prison.

I certainly don't see myself as the equal of St. Paul. My point is that perhaps there are times when God uses our tragedies to serve a greater good. I like to tell myself that. Having endured what we endured, Renee, John and I may be helping a great many families other than our own, people we'll never meet.

That's the thing about surviving the lingering death of the person you love most. It leaves you wondering and wandering. Not much seems certain.

All of us are capable of nobility and selfishness alike. We're all imperfect.

This much I've learned from my experiences: the best you can do in life is the best you can do. If there were any advice I could pass on to others, it would be this: just do your best. Try to forgive others for whatever fault they've laid to their own account, or have laid to yours, and try to forgive yourself. Then keep pressing forward.